PRIVATE LESSONS

SALSA HANON

By Peter Deneff

ISBN 978-0-7935-8494-9

7777 W. BLUEMOUND RD. P.O. BOX 13819 MILWAUKEE, WI 53213

Visit Hal Leonard Online at
www.halleonard.com

Acknowledgements

I'd like to thank the following people who have been a great influence and inspiration to me: My parents, George V. Deneff, and Alkisti Deneff. My teachers, Leaine Gibson and Mike Garson. Their incredible knowledge and wisdom continue to amaze and inspire me. My children, Gitana, George, and Sophia. They are my greatest joy and my biggest fans. My wife, Diane Azzara. She continues to believe in me and support my art (even though the rewards are often slim). I am thankful that she is my wife, soul mate, and mother of my children. Besides that, she actually thinks my jokes are funny...

Finally, I would like to dedicate this book to my father, George V. Deneff. Although he is no longer among us, his wisdom continues to guide me.

Contents

About the author

Peter Deneff grew up in Long Beach, California listening to Greek and classical music and studying classical piano with Leaine Gibson. After starting his professional life playing in a Greek wedding band at age fifteen, he became obsessed with straight-ahead and Latin jazz. He began jazz studies with renowned pianist Mike Garson, where he crafted his art through studying some of the great jazz improvisers such as Charlie Parker, Bud Powell, and Chick Corea. During this time he also studied many ethnic styles that eventually led to the development of his classical and jazz compositional style as well as the formation of his Middle Eastern-Latin jazz group *Excursion* (*www.excursionjazz.com*). He also pursued undergraduate and graduate studies in classical composition and film scoring at California State University Long Beach under the direction of Dr. Justus Matthews, Dr. Martin Herman and Perry Lamarca. Peter has written several best-selling books for Hal Leonard Corporation including *Blues Hanon, Guitar Hanon, Jazz Chord Hanon, Jazz Hanon, Rock Hanon, Salsa Hanon, Samba Hanon,* and *Stride Hanon.* He has also composed and performed music for the Charles Sheen film, *Five Aces.* Deneff has performed at such varied venues as the Greek Theater, the Carpenter Performing Arts Center, the Playboy Jazz Festival, the Los Angeles Street Scene, the Orange County Street Fair, Universal Studios, the NAMM show, and the Baked Potato. His stylistic versatility has allowed him to play and/or sing with a diverse assortment of groups like Tierra, Ike Willis (singer with Frank Zappa), the Leslie Paula/Universal Studios Salsa Band, and Ebi, a notable Persian singer. Deneff also continues to play and record modern and folk Greek music for numerous events (*www.synthesimusic.com*) as well as an occasional Middle Eastern or jazz gig. Besides performing, Peter has also taught in many institutions such as Musician's Institute, Orange County High School of the Arts, and Cypress College, where he continues to teach classical and jazz piano. He spends most of his time in his studio producing projects for Yamaha Corporation (*Disklavier, Clavinova, Internet Direct Content*) and Hal Leonard Corporation (*PVG Play-Alongs, Instrumental Play-Alongs*).

Introduction

Latin jazz and salsa are wonderfully intricate, challenging, and enjoyable styles of music. Besides being harmonically interesting, they are quite complicated rhythmically and therefore require specialized technique from a performing musician. Being a percussion-based style, salsa demands the same rhythmic ferocity and percussive touch from the pianist as it does from from the conga or timbale player. The syncopated rhythms of Latin music are not necessarily left up to the player's discretion, however; in order for the ensemble to work properly, all the players must understand their place within the detailed tapestry of the rhythm.

Specifically, the pianist must be rhythmically and technically capable enough to play "montunos," which are distinctive rhythmic motives that serve as a major driving force in the Latin orchestra. There are technical challenges that exist in the execution of montunos that are unique to salsa—these include a heavy reliance on the fifth finger (a finger that is naturally weak), because there is so much octave playing.

This book is intended as a sort of Latin sequel to Charles Louis Hanon's *The Virtuoso Pianist in Sixty Exercises*, a classic of piano literature that has been pushing pianists' technique to the limit for over one hundred years. When *this* book is mastered, you will be able to execute practically any Latin montuno pattern. The exercises in this book are perfect for either the beginner or the professional and can even benefit pianists of other genres such as jazz or classical. They may be practiced as quickly as they can be played cleanly and accurately. Some tips that I like to keep in mind when practicing these exercises include the following:

- Start very slowly, deliberately, and staccato. This builds articulation.

- Use a metronome. The metronome will help you develop your sense of time.

- When you master an exercise at a given speed, increase the tempo one notch on your metronome.

- Keep your fingers curved.

- Don't tense up.

- Push yourself, but stop if it hurts!

These exercises should be learned in all twelve keys because it is important to feel at ease anywhere on the keyboard. Also, you should try to play them in harmonic, melodic, and natural minor. Meanwhile, it is important to listen to great Latin music in order to absorb the feeling of the music—some of my favorite Latin players are listed in the back of this book.

Included in this edition is a CD of complete backing tracks which are intended to enhance your practicing experience. The tempo of these audio tracks can be adjusted with the included software. Because many of the rhythms are very intricate, it is important to count carefully and practice at a reasonable tempo.

The main thing to remember is to have fun with these exercises, be creative, and find new ways to incorporate these techniques into your music, Latin or not. Last but not least, do not get discouraged. Technique doesn't happen overnight; it may take weeks or even months to master some of these exercises. It will certainly take longer to master them in all keys. Pace yourself, and you will succeed in mastering this book and be well on your way to becoming the next great Latin pianist!

Happy playing,
Peter Deneff

Single-Voice Montuno Exercises

1

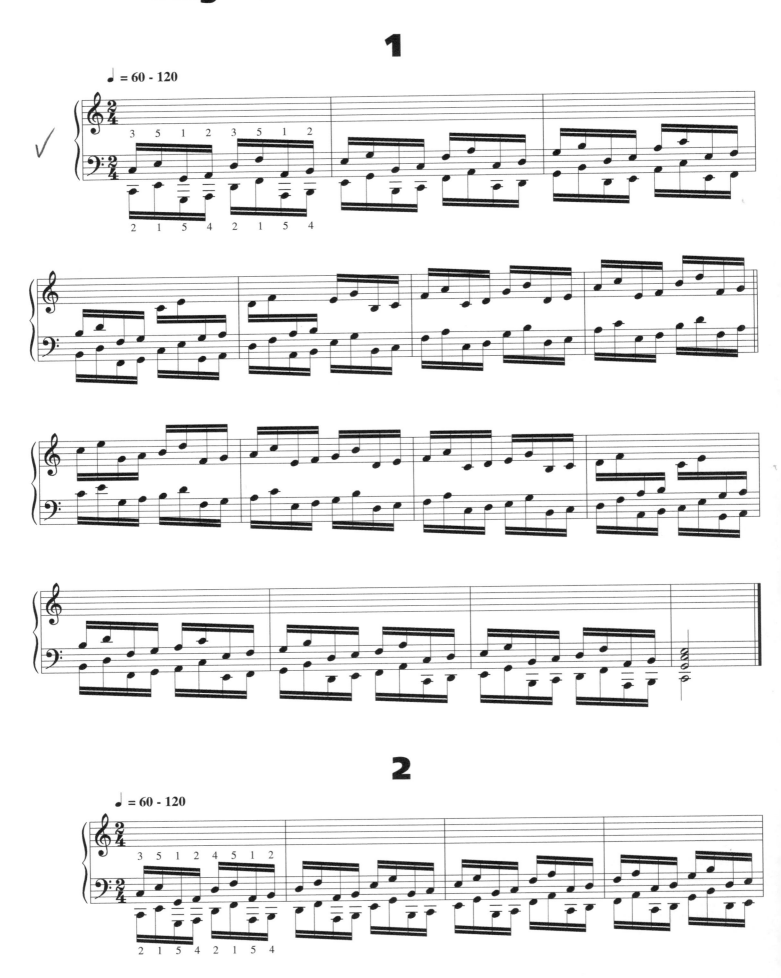

2

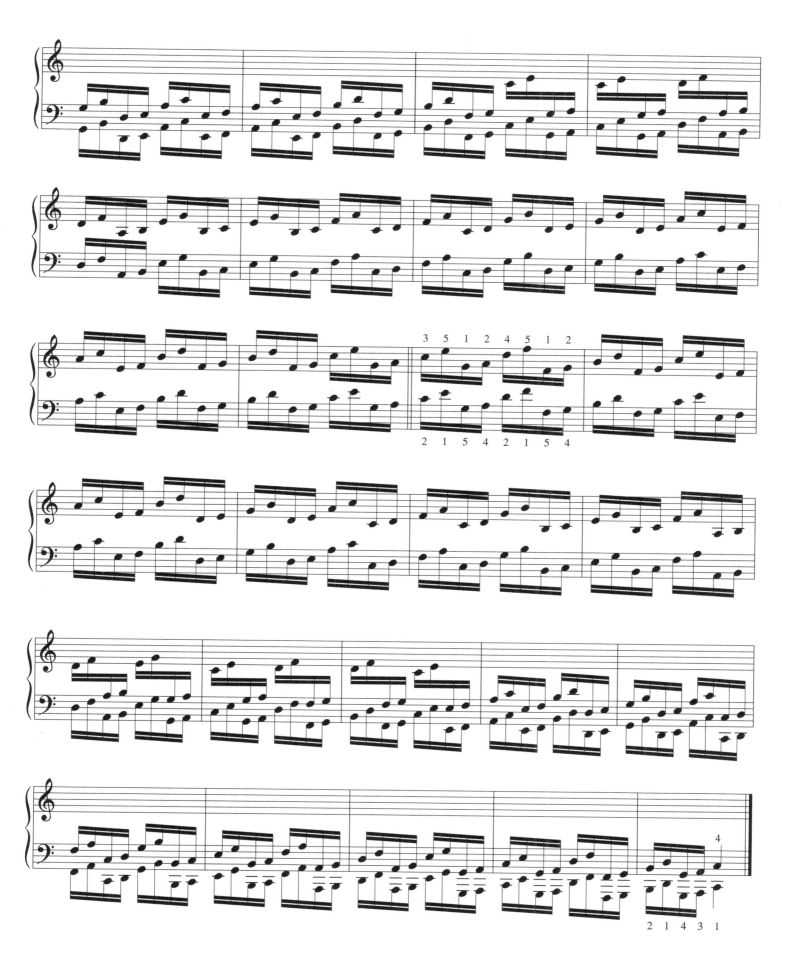

3

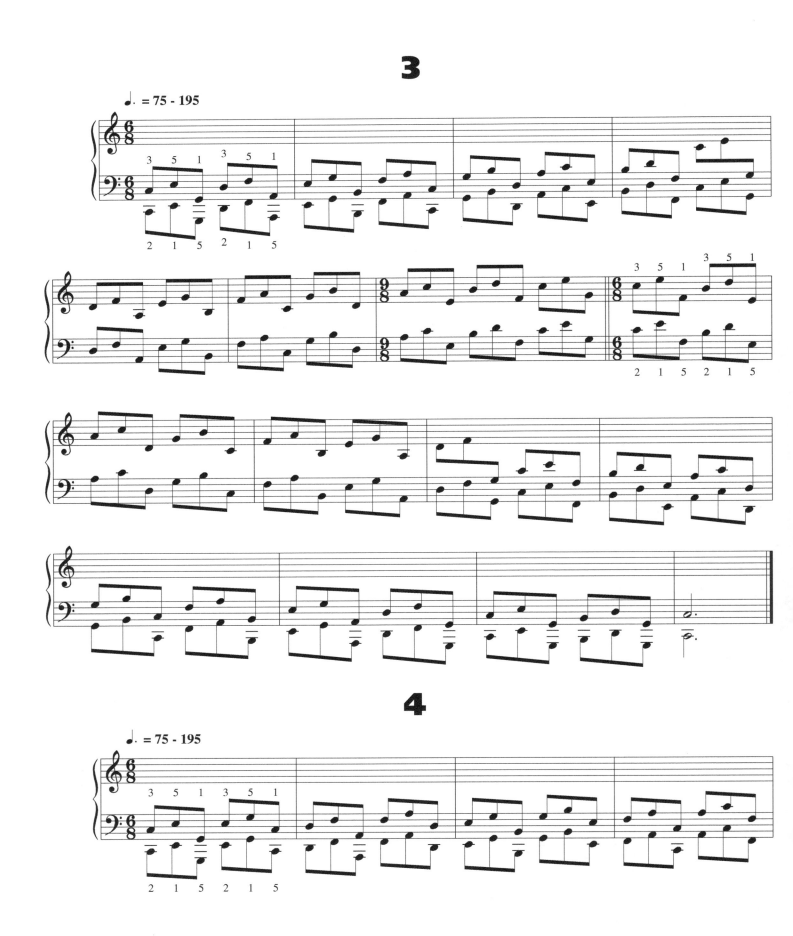

4

5

Variations of the Single-Voice Montuno
Exercises Using Syncopation

6

7

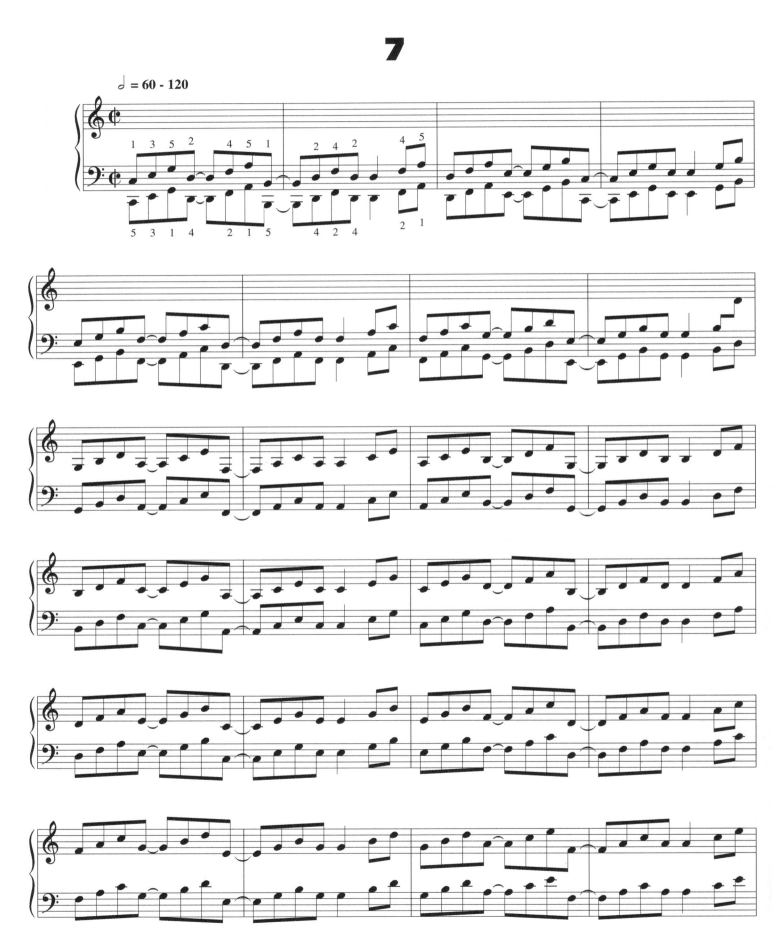

8

9

10

Octave Montuno Exercises
Grouped in Threes

11

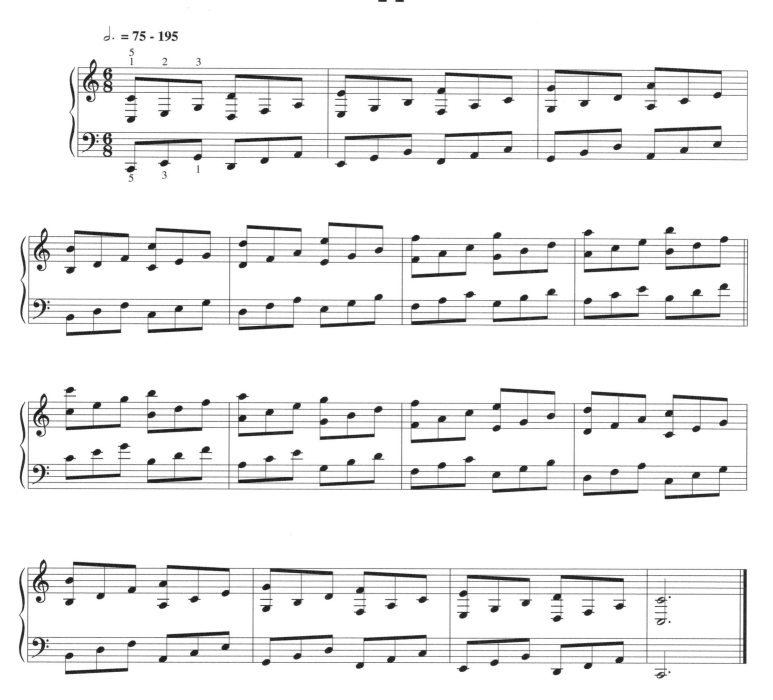

12

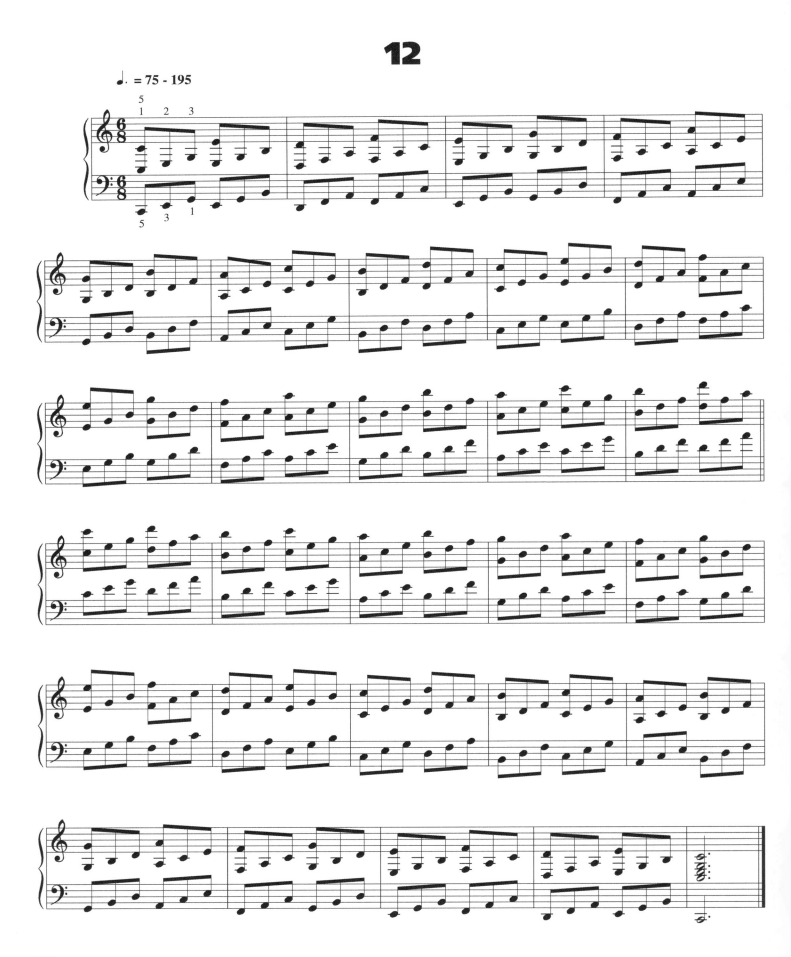

13

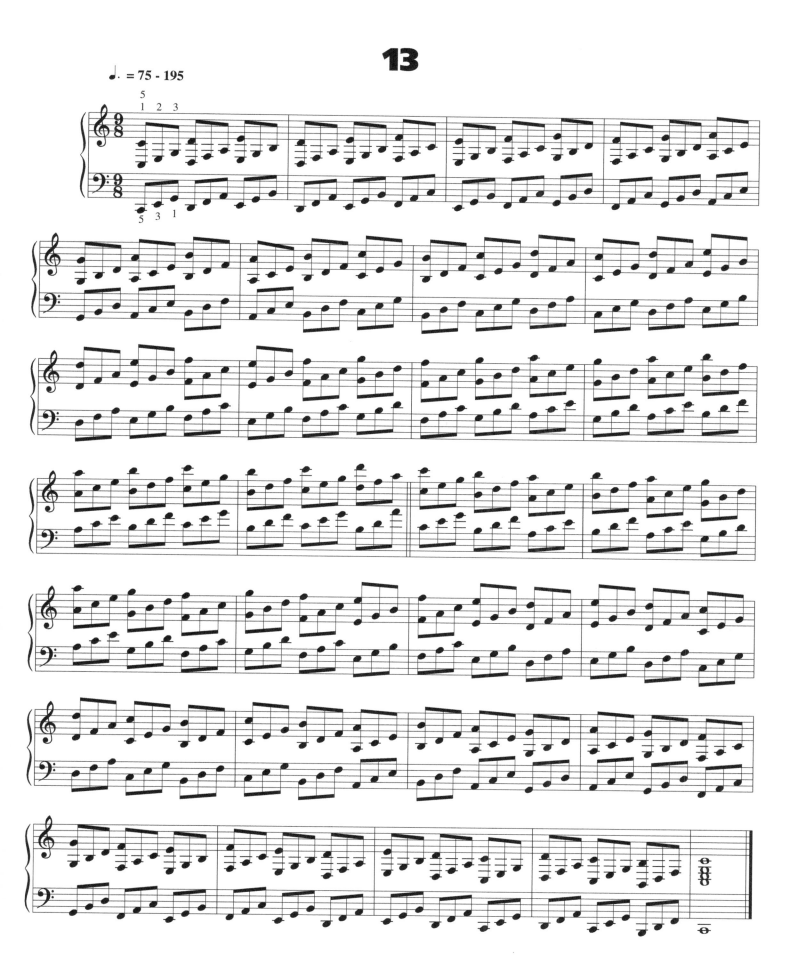

14

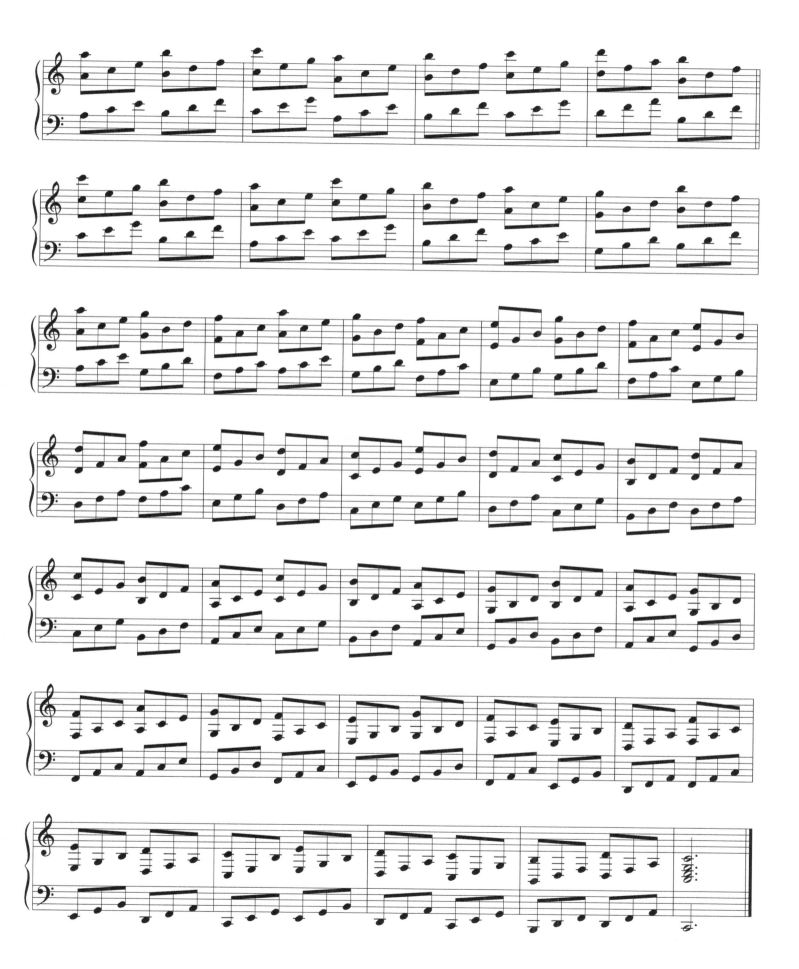

15

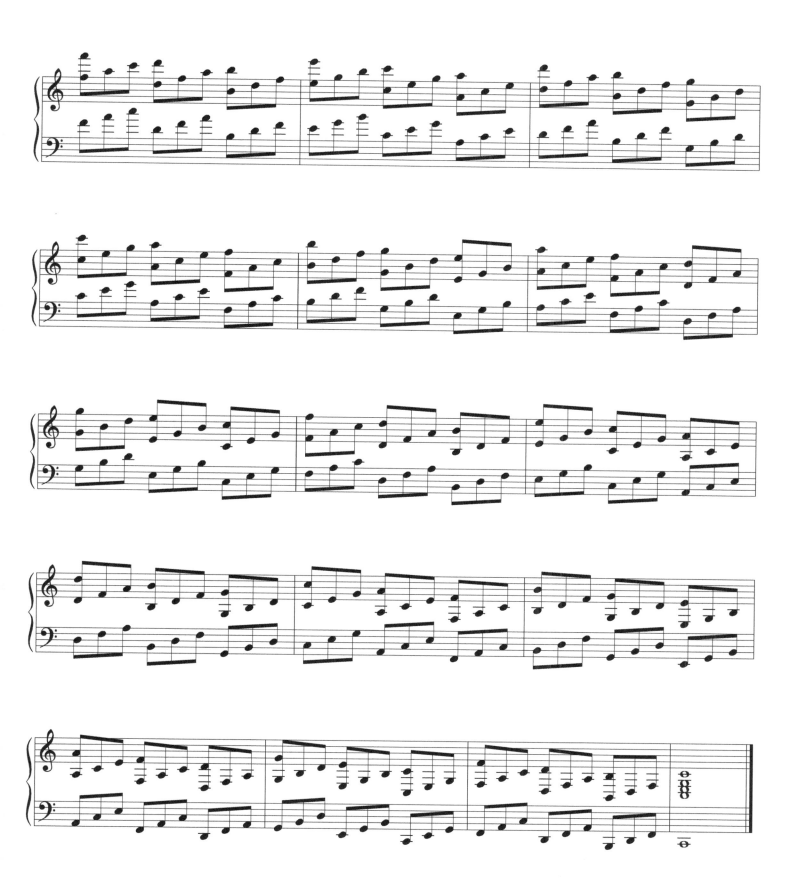

16

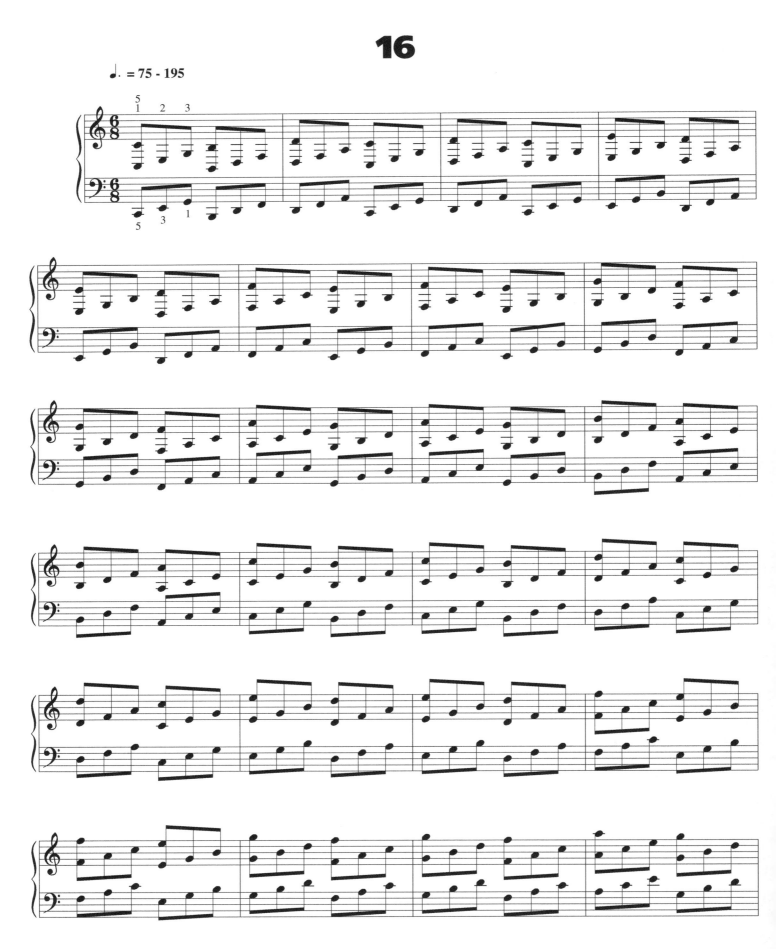

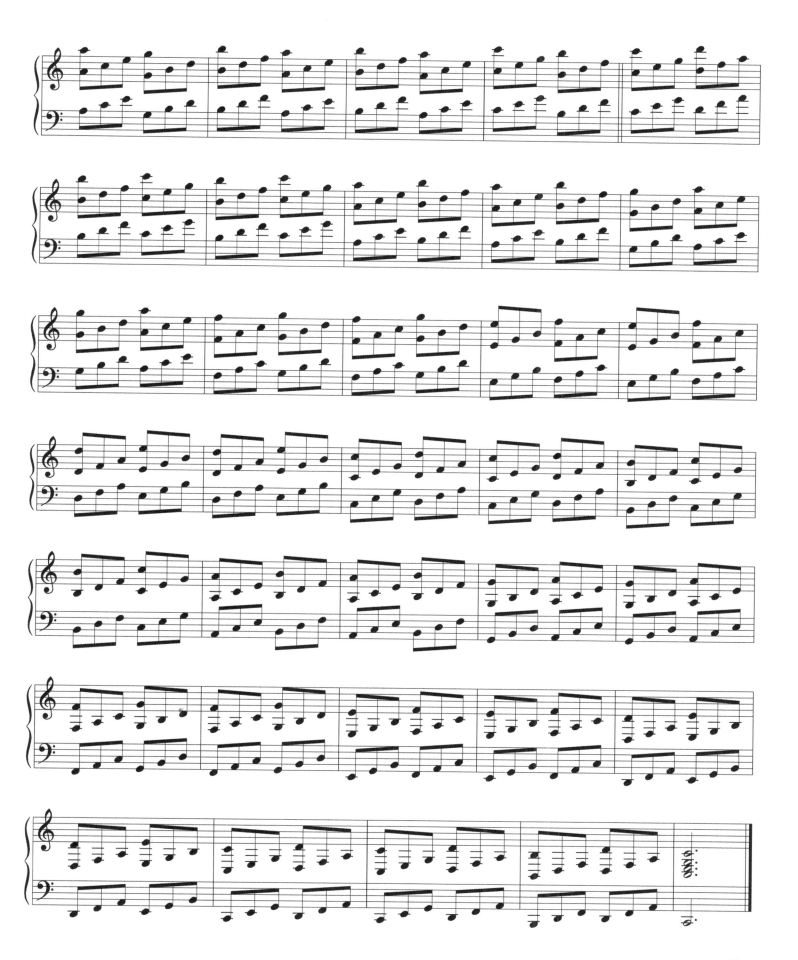

17

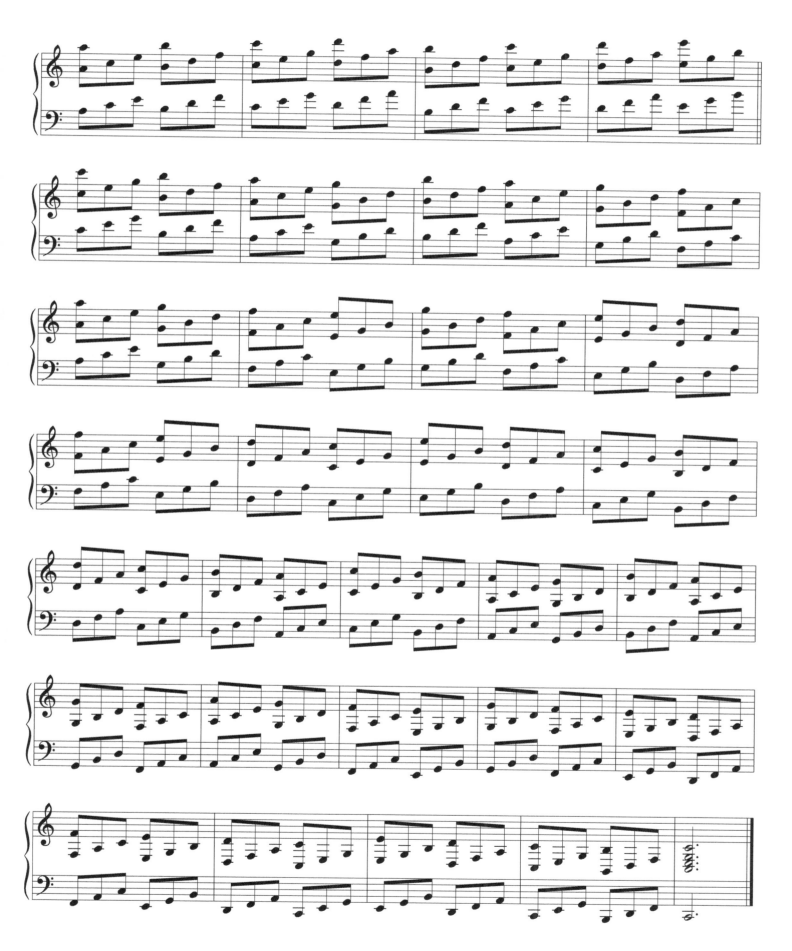

18

♩. = 75 - 195

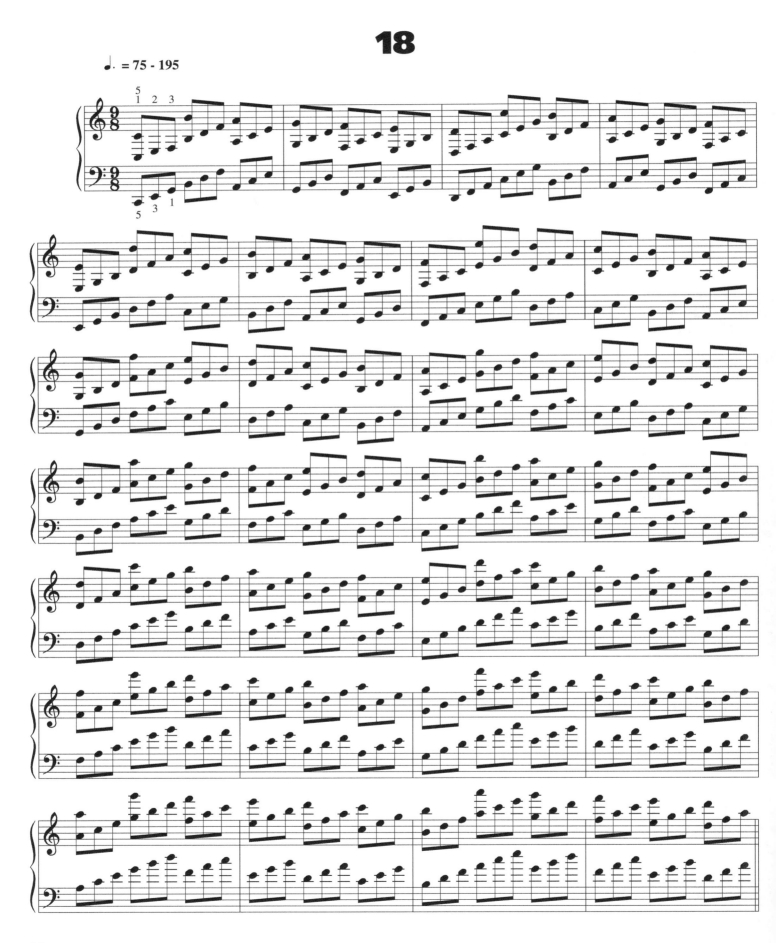

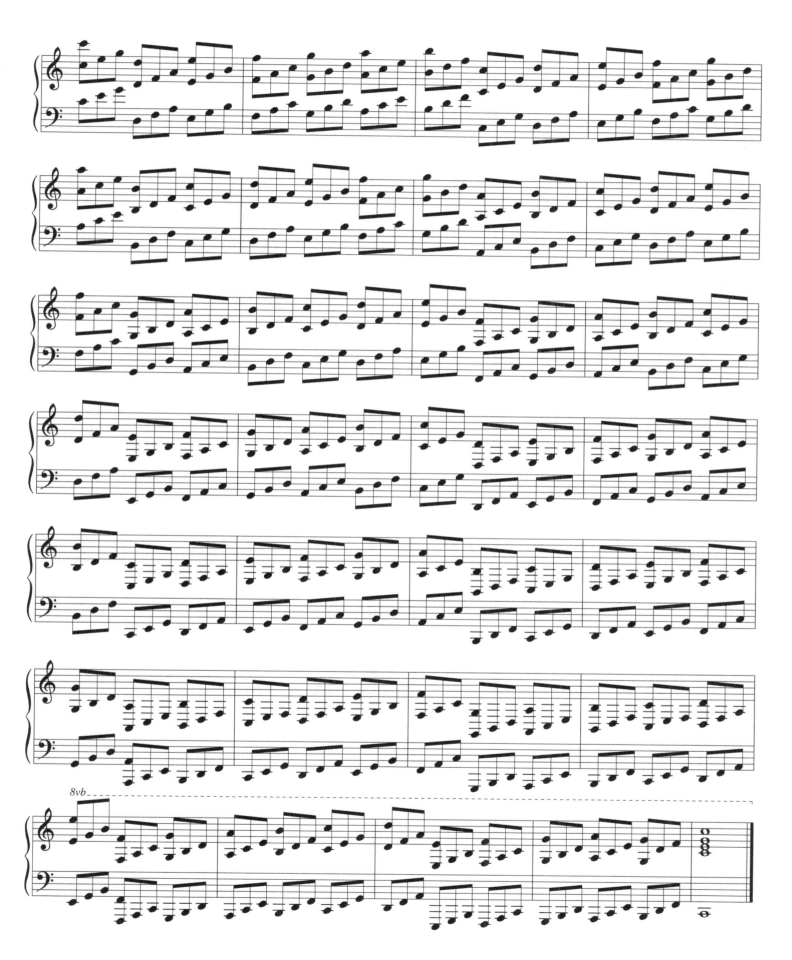

19

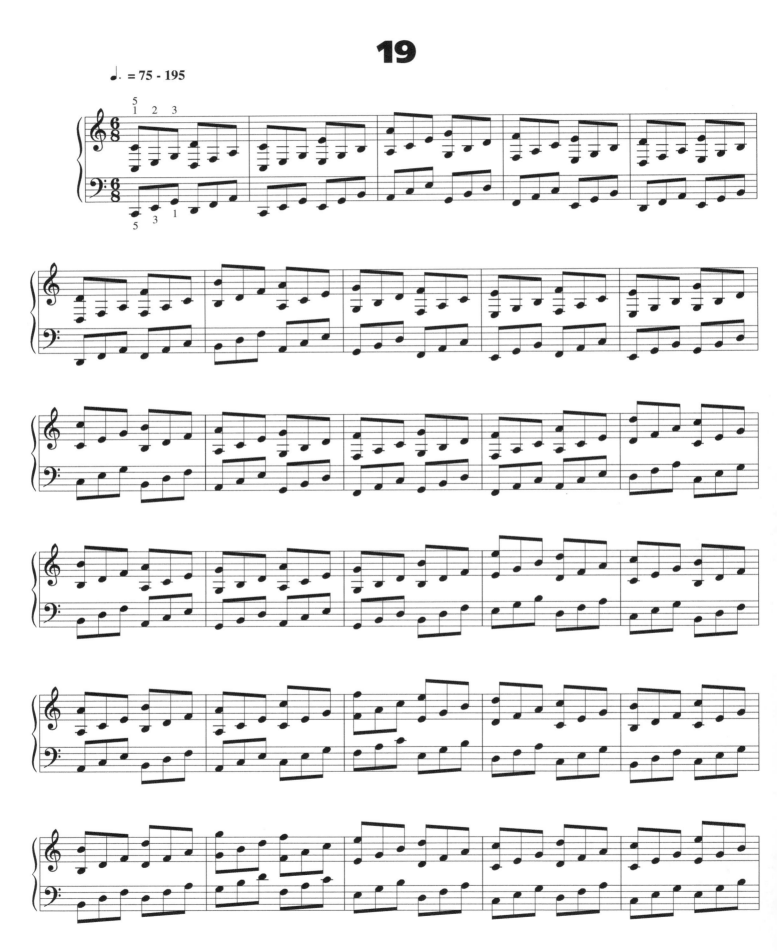

20

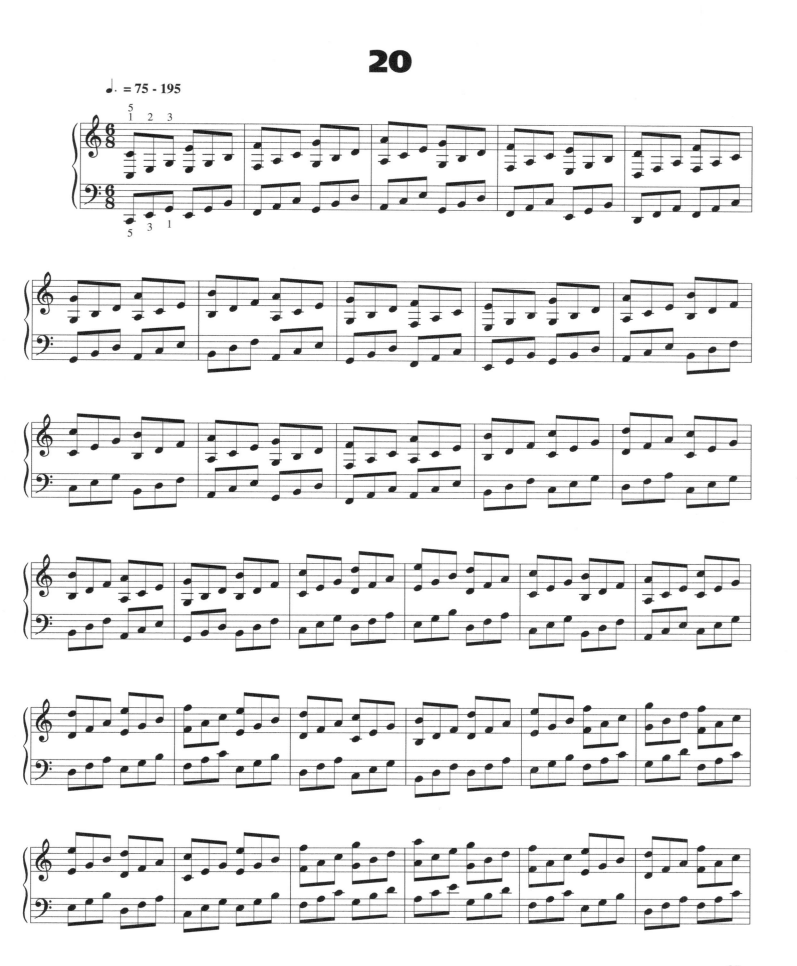

Octave Montuno Exercises
Harmonized in Tenths

21

22

23

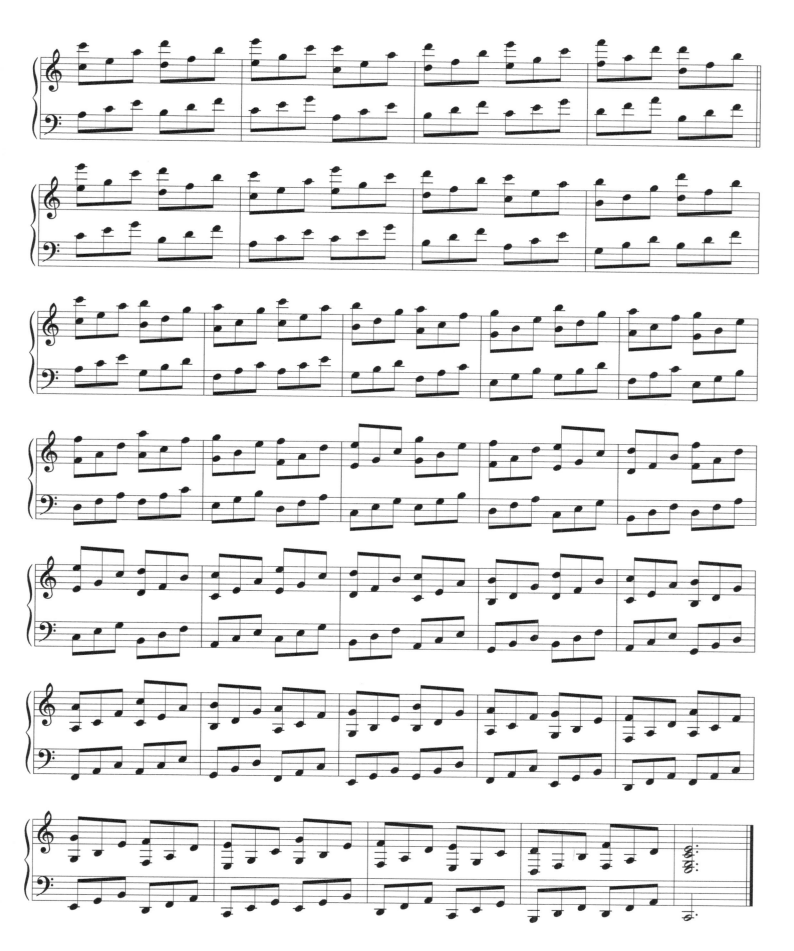

24

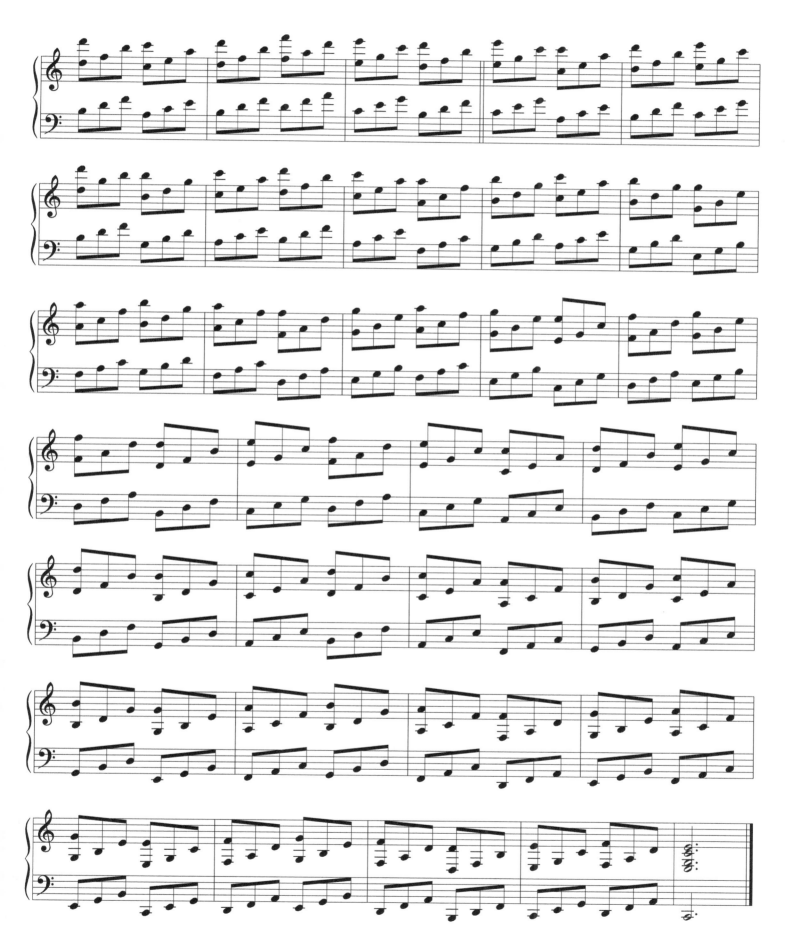

25

26

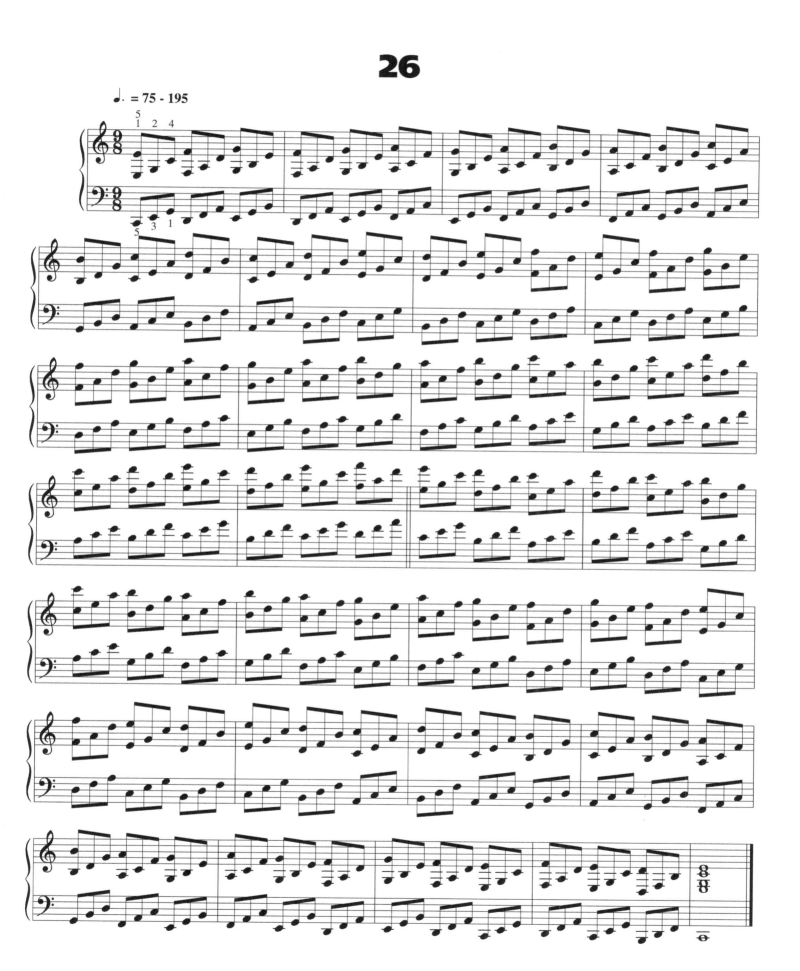

27

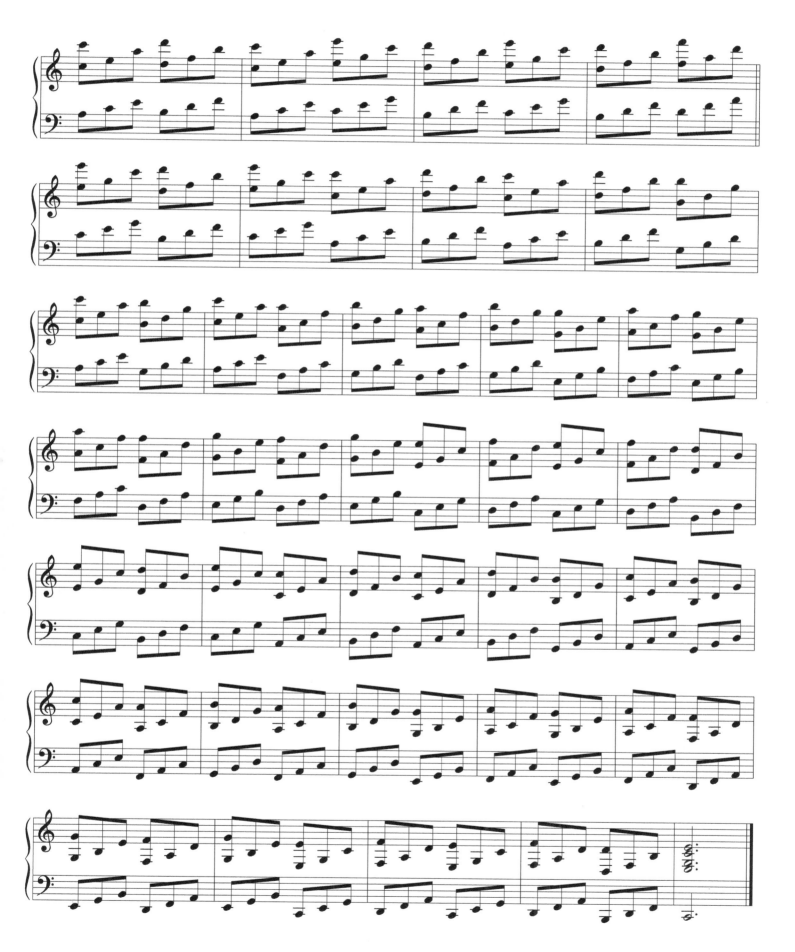

28

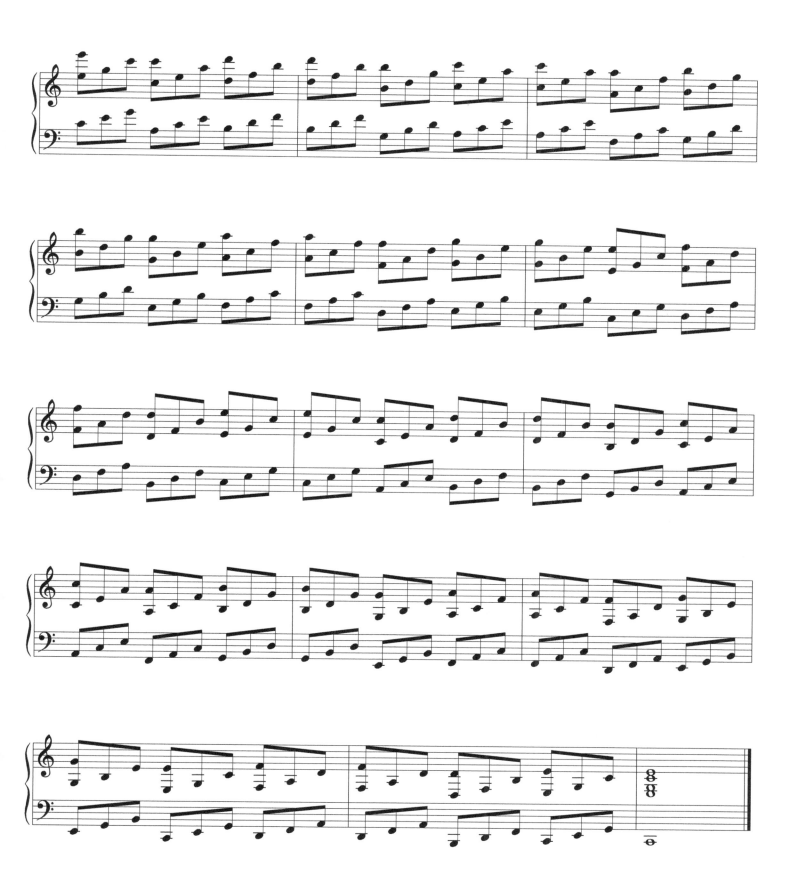

29

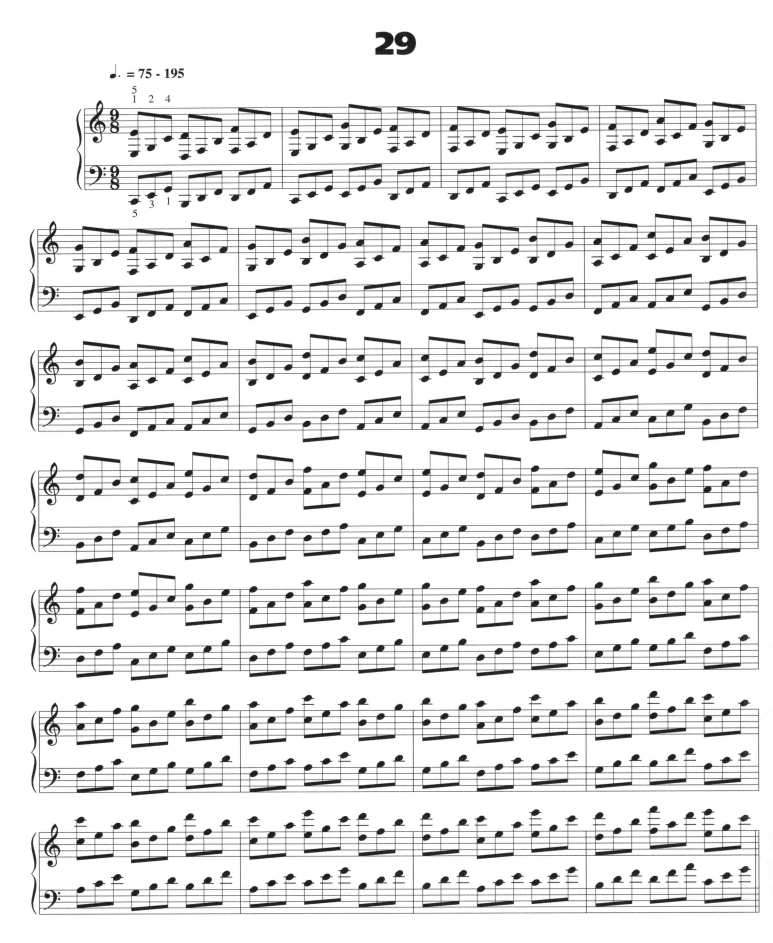

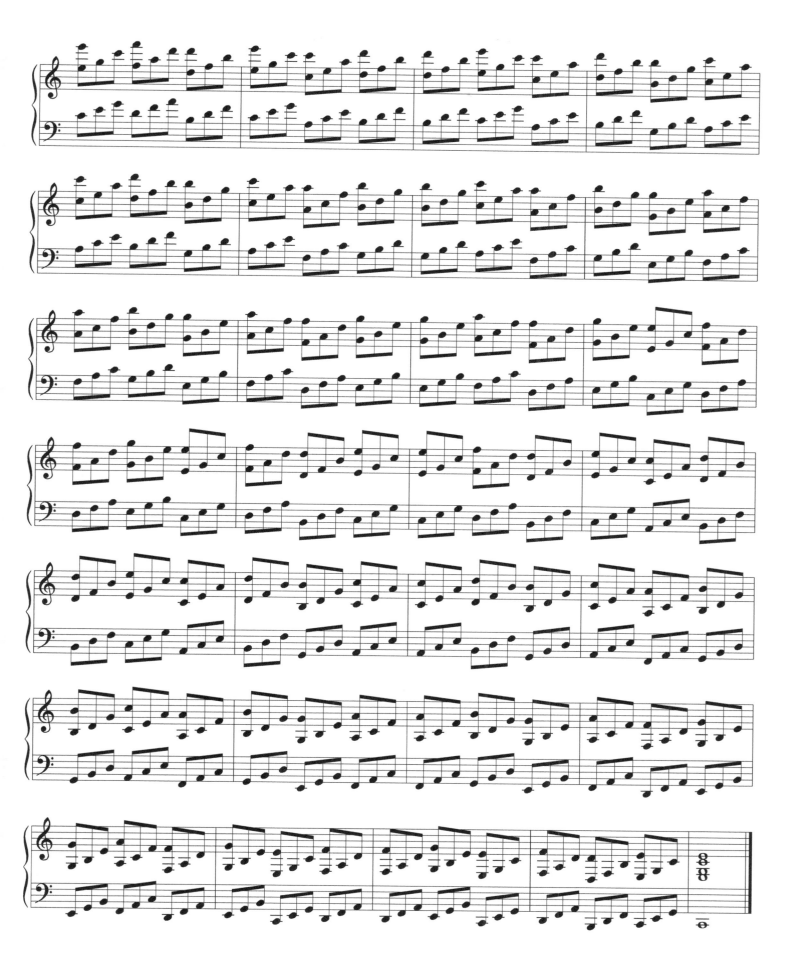

30

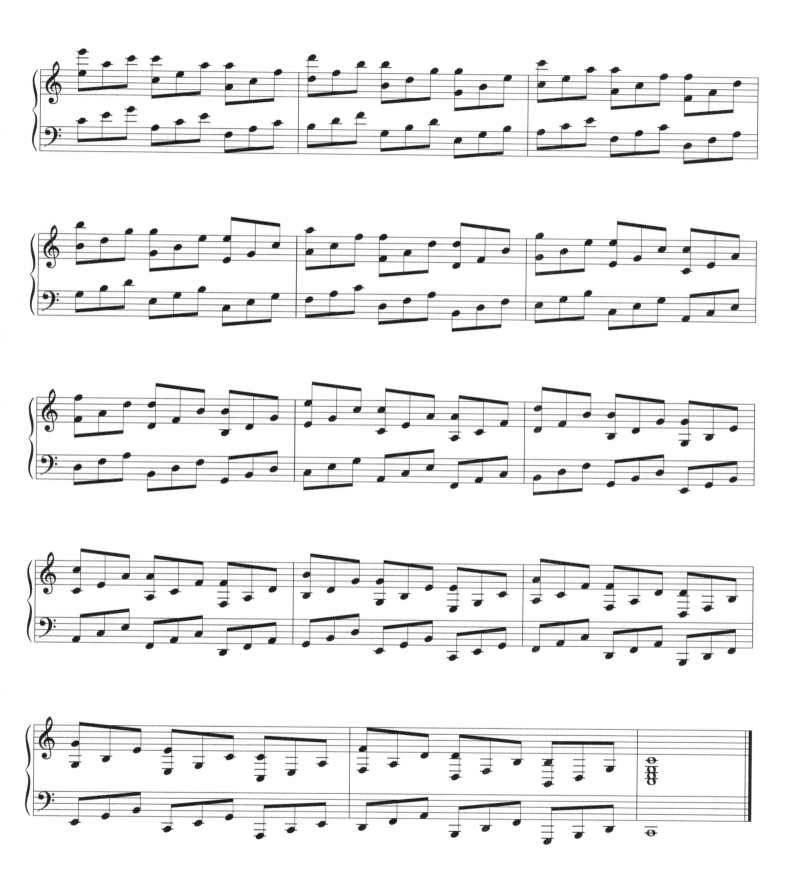

Octave Montuno Exercises
Grouped in Fours

31

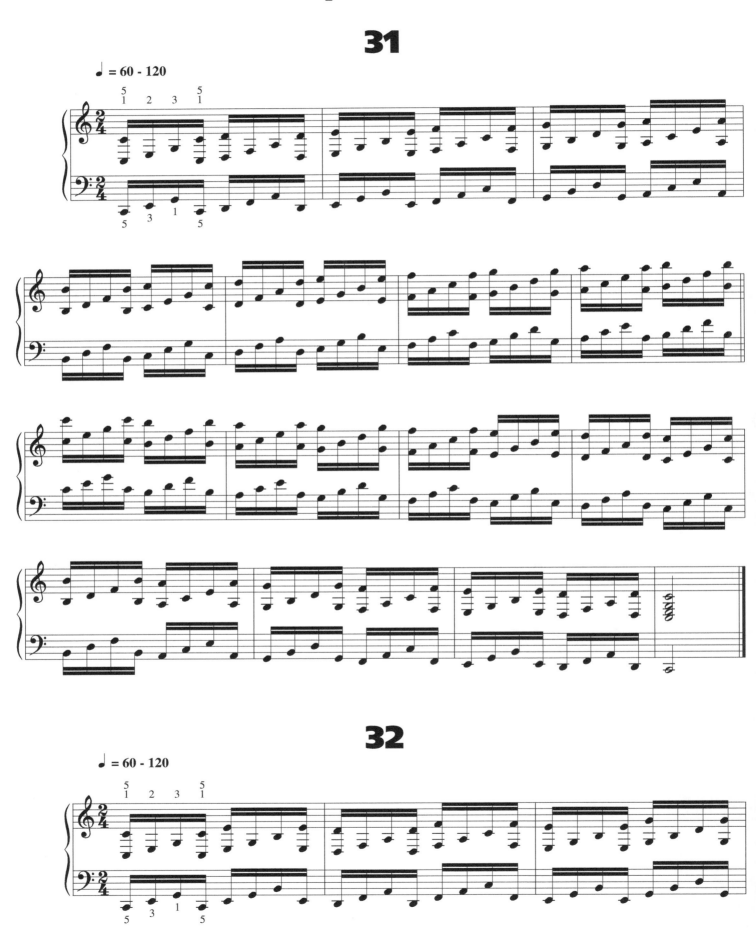

32

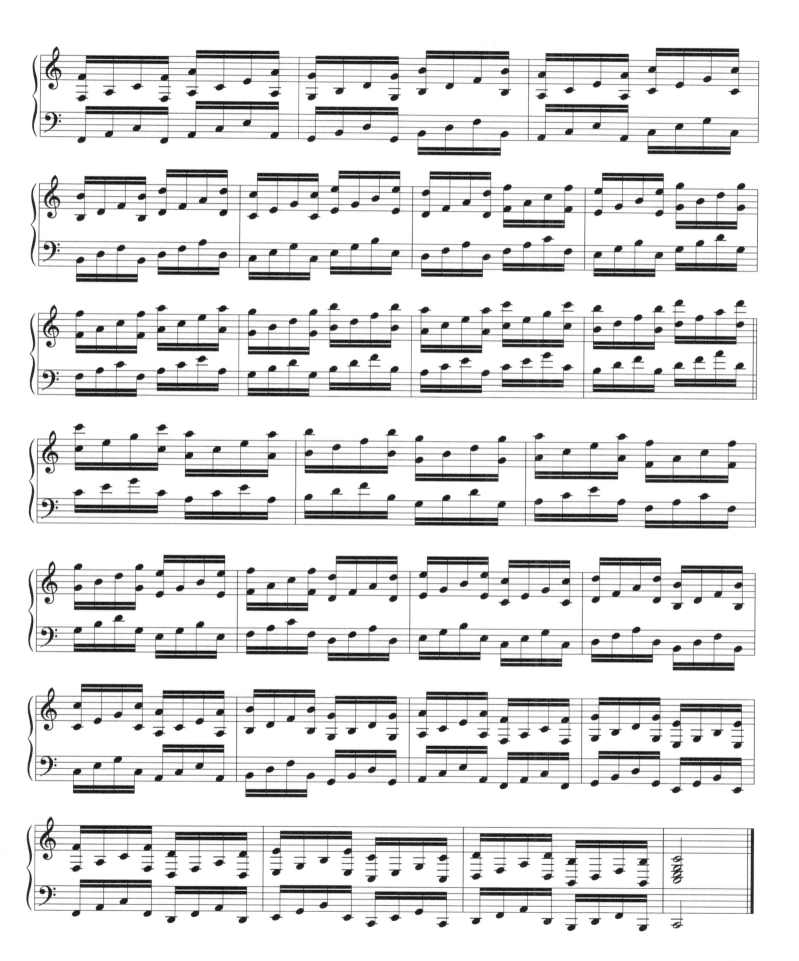

33

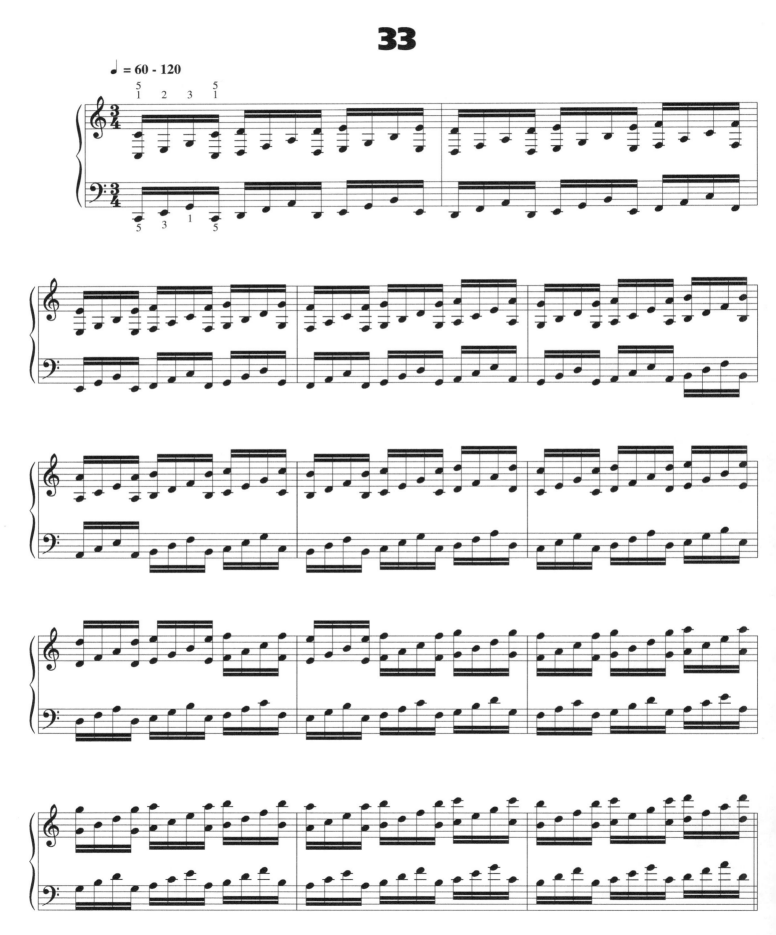

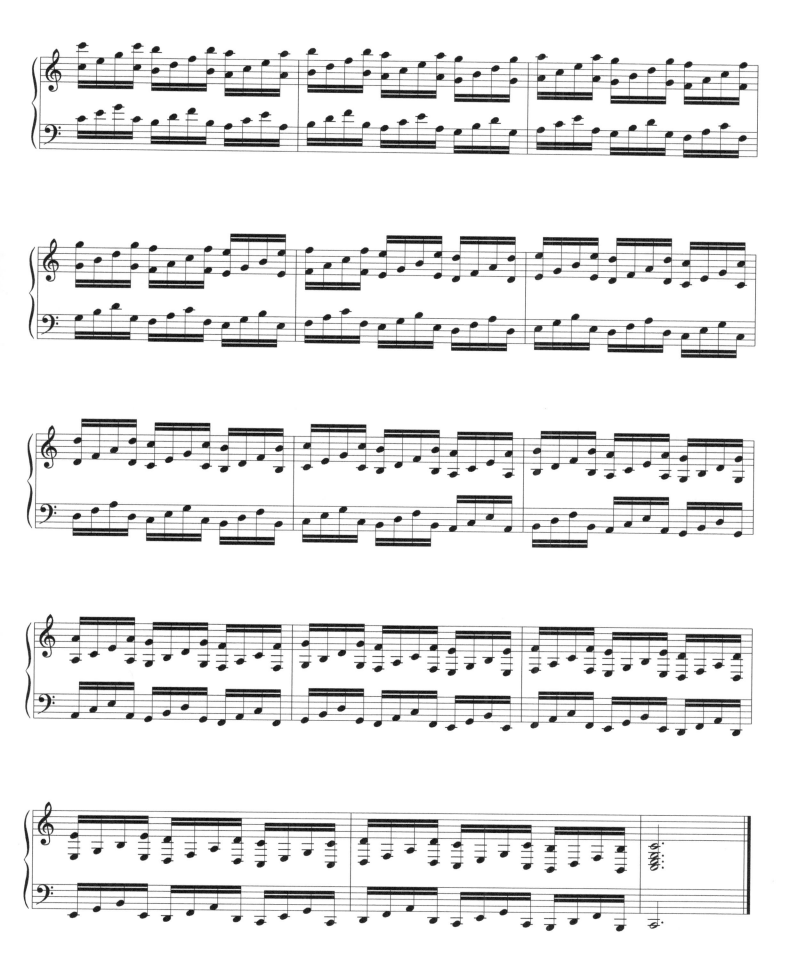

34

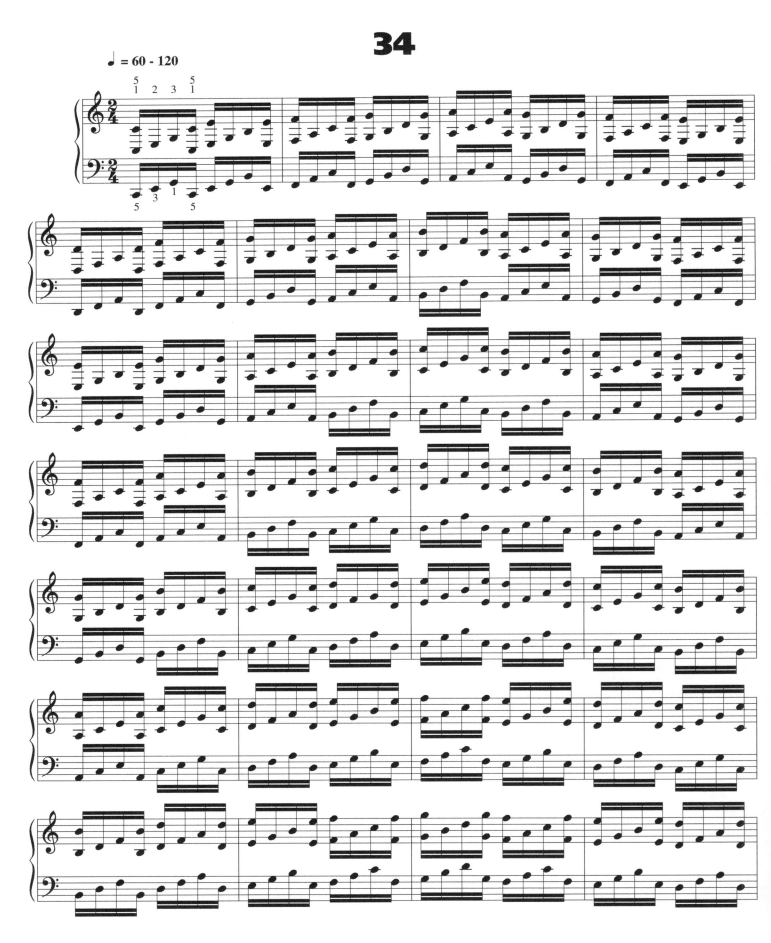

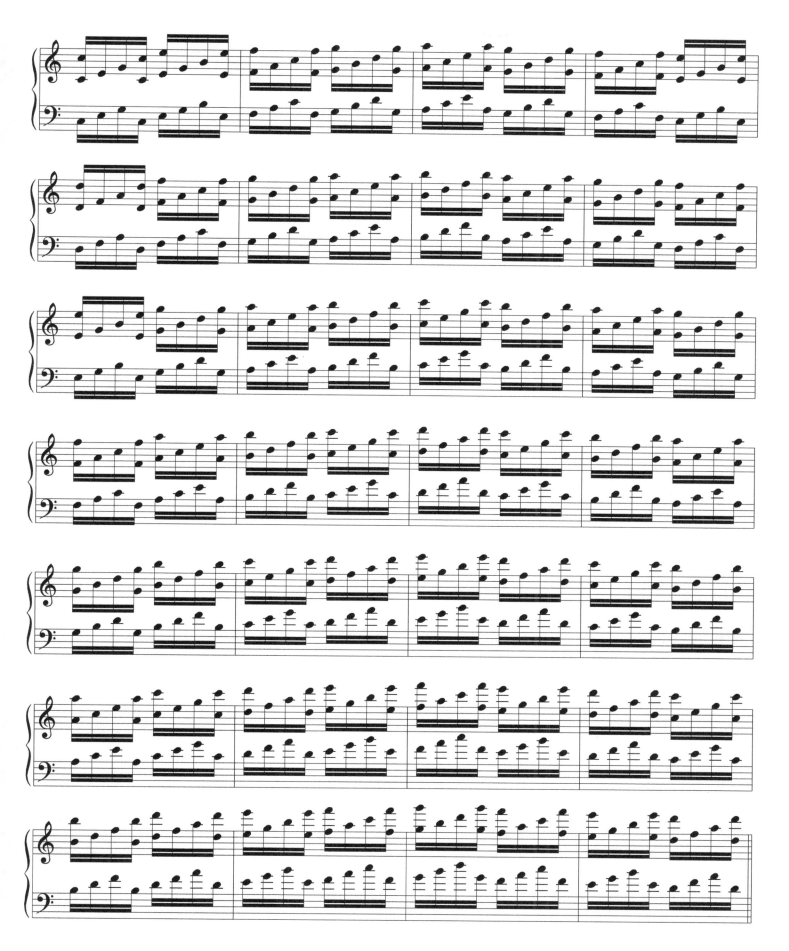

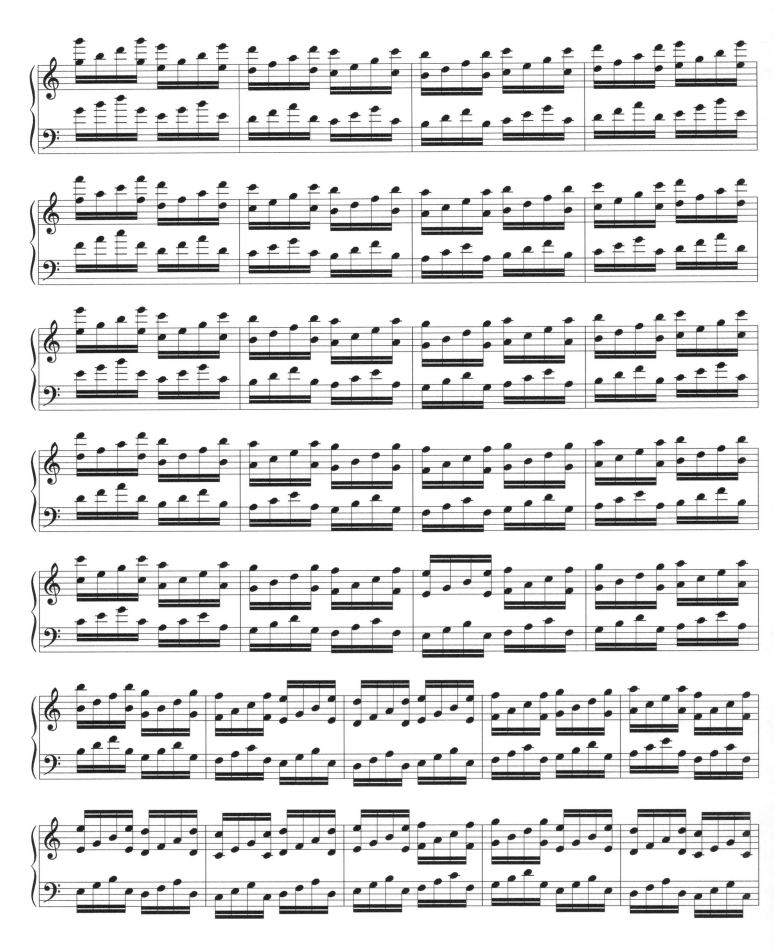

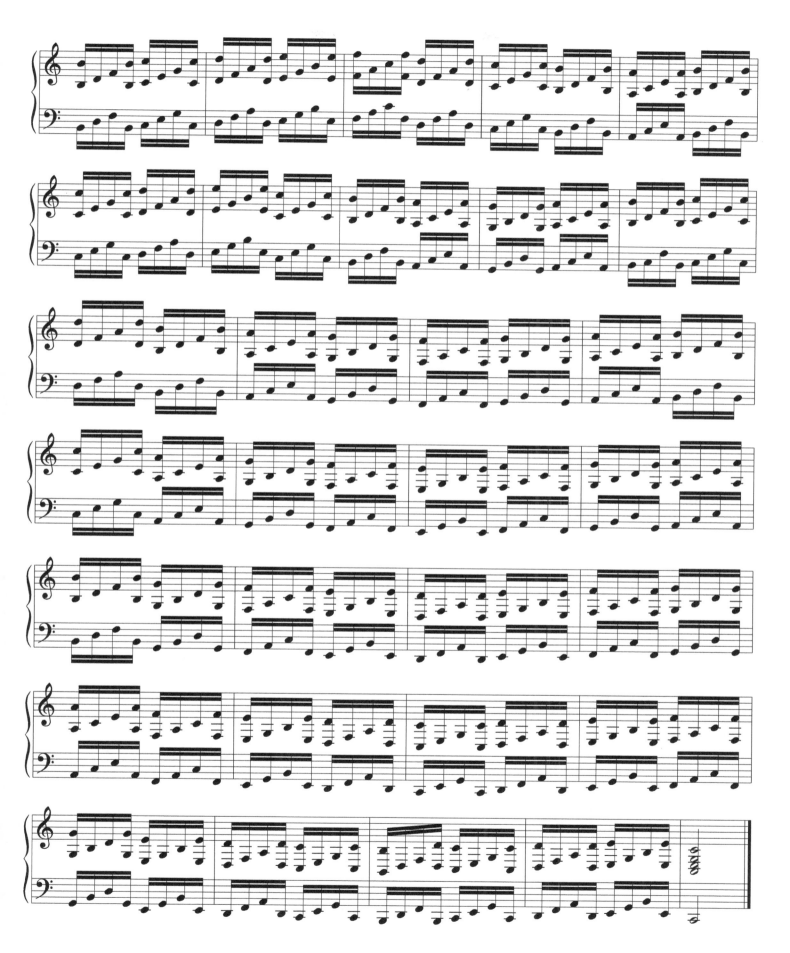

35

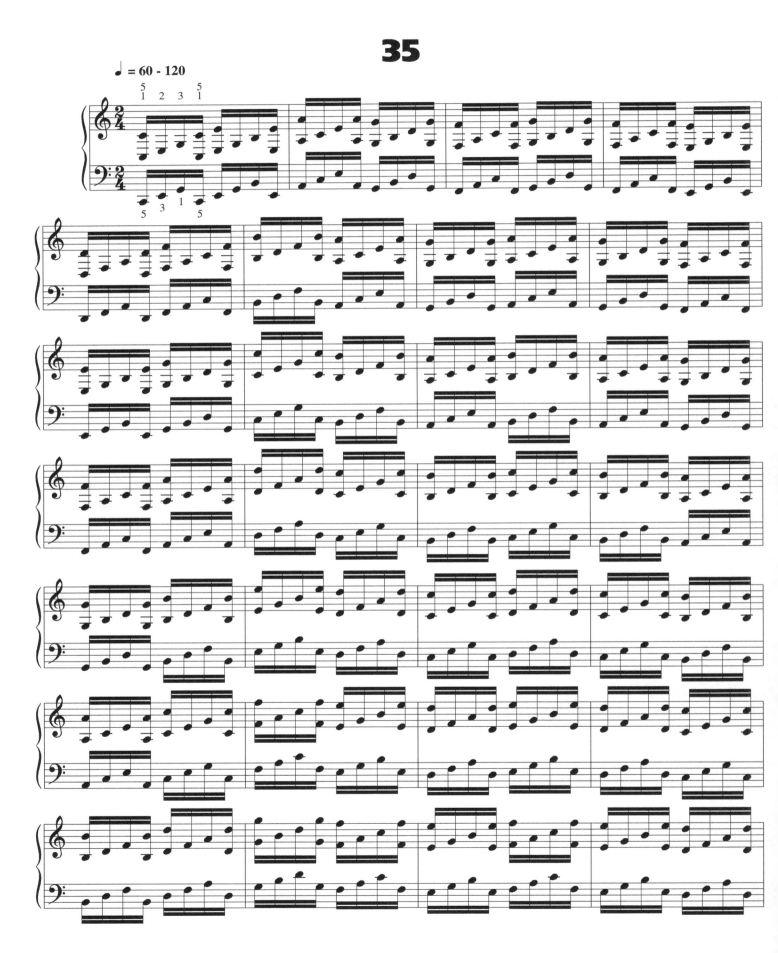

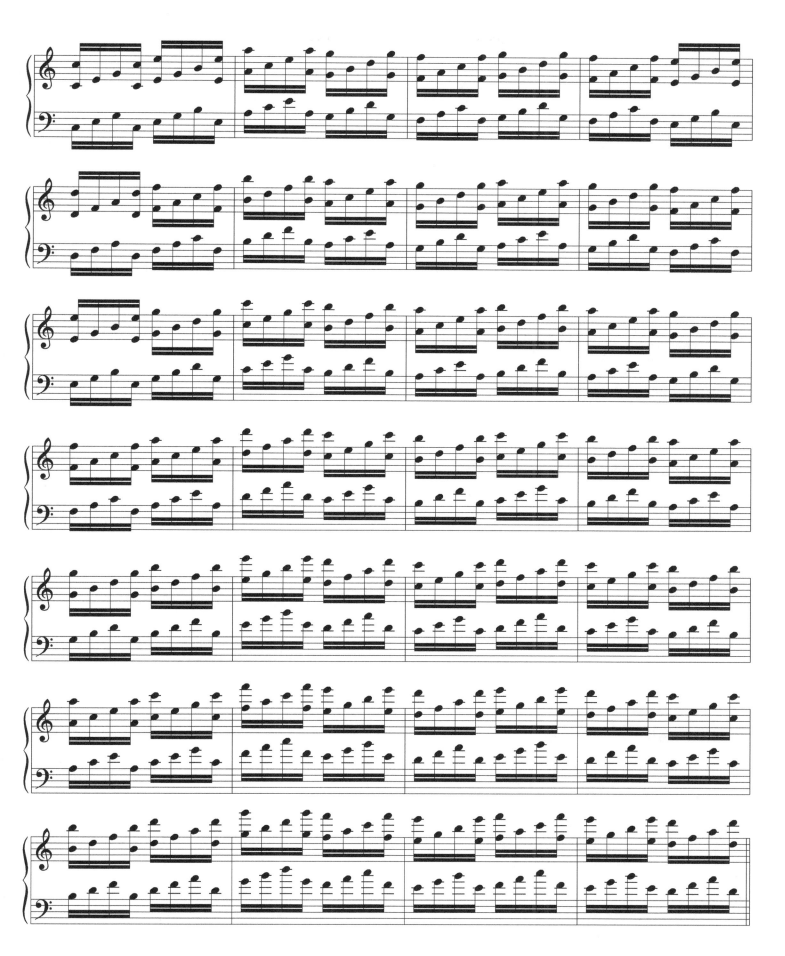

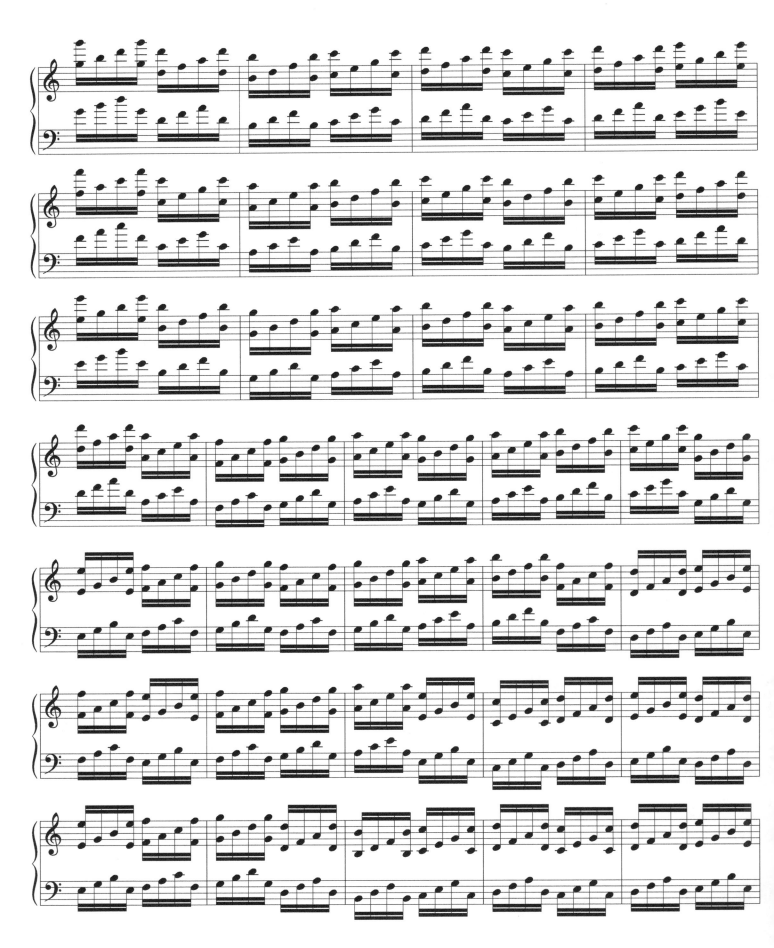

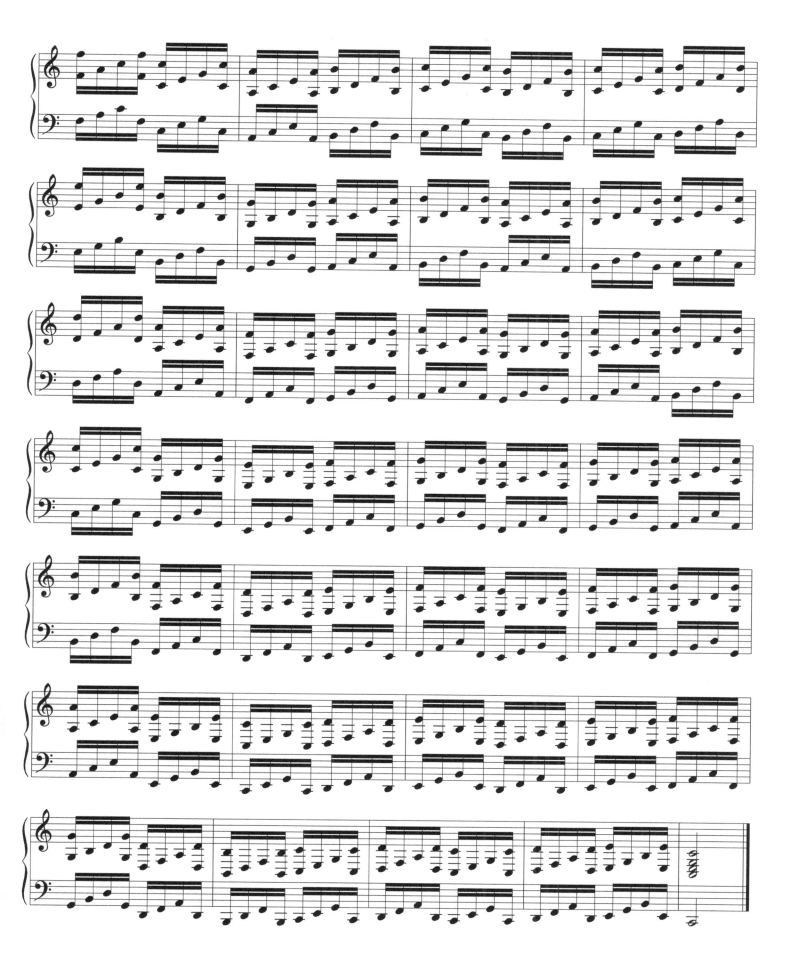

36

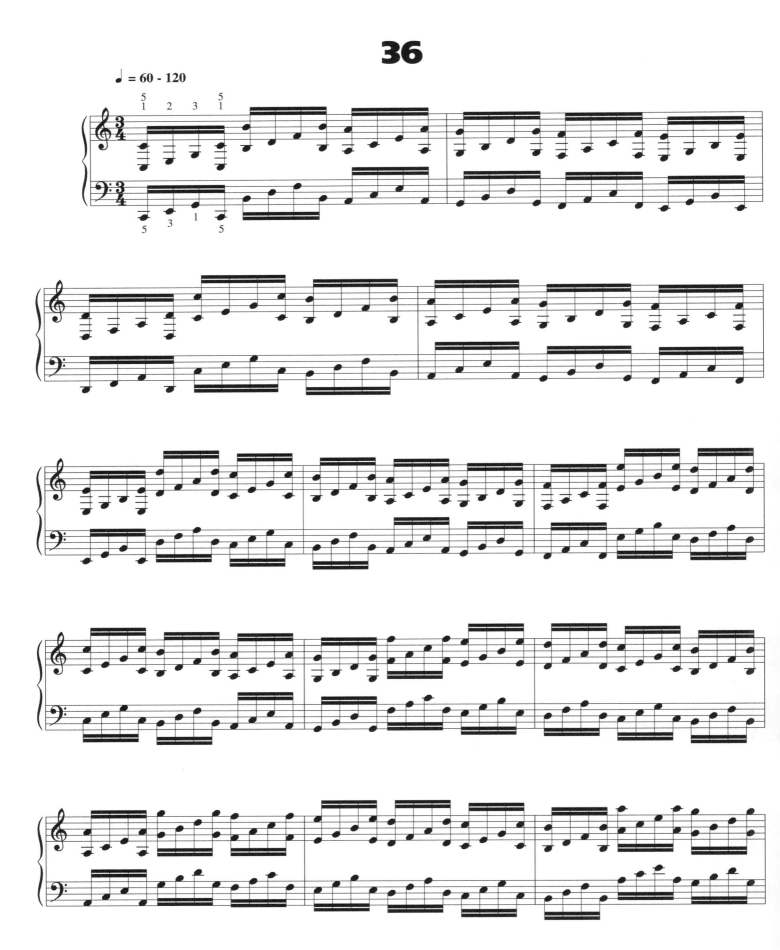

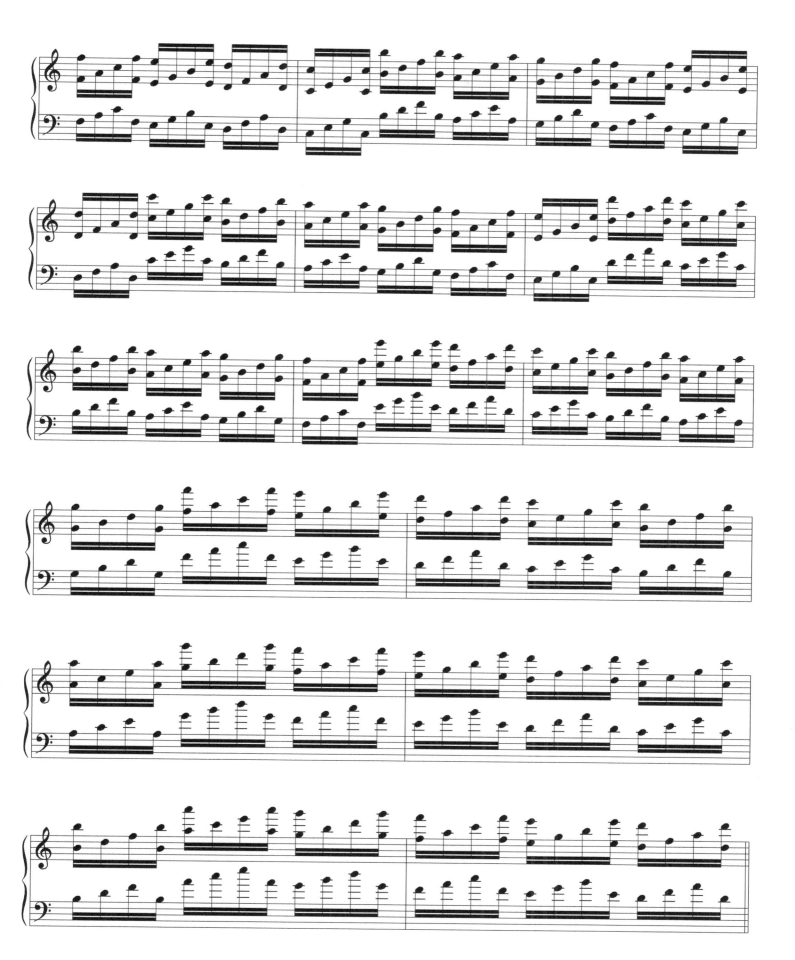

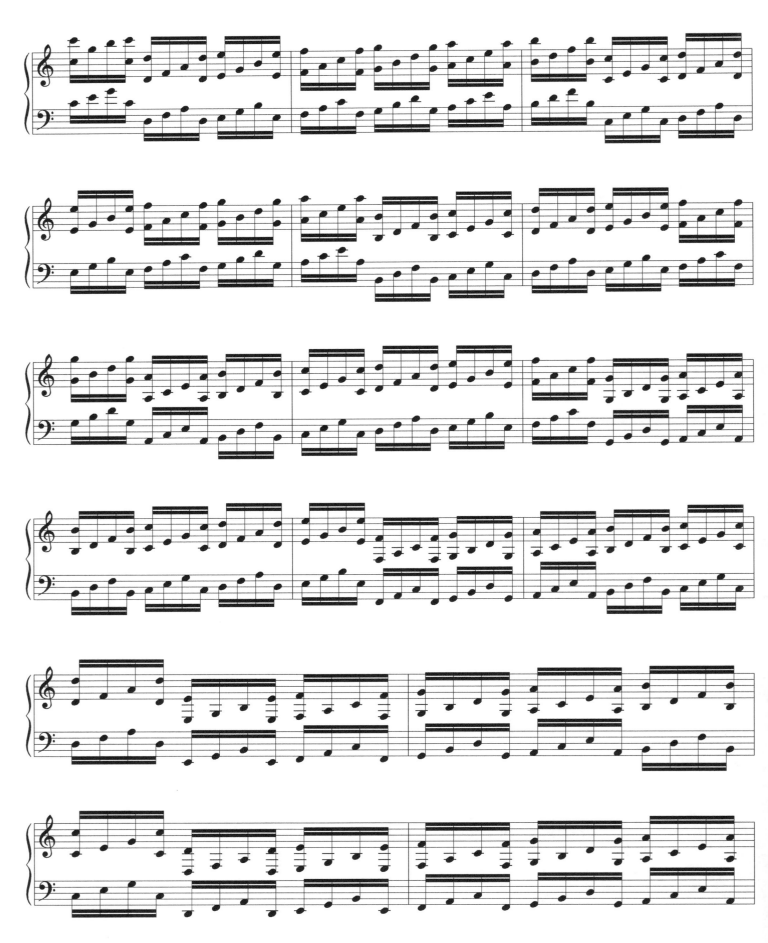

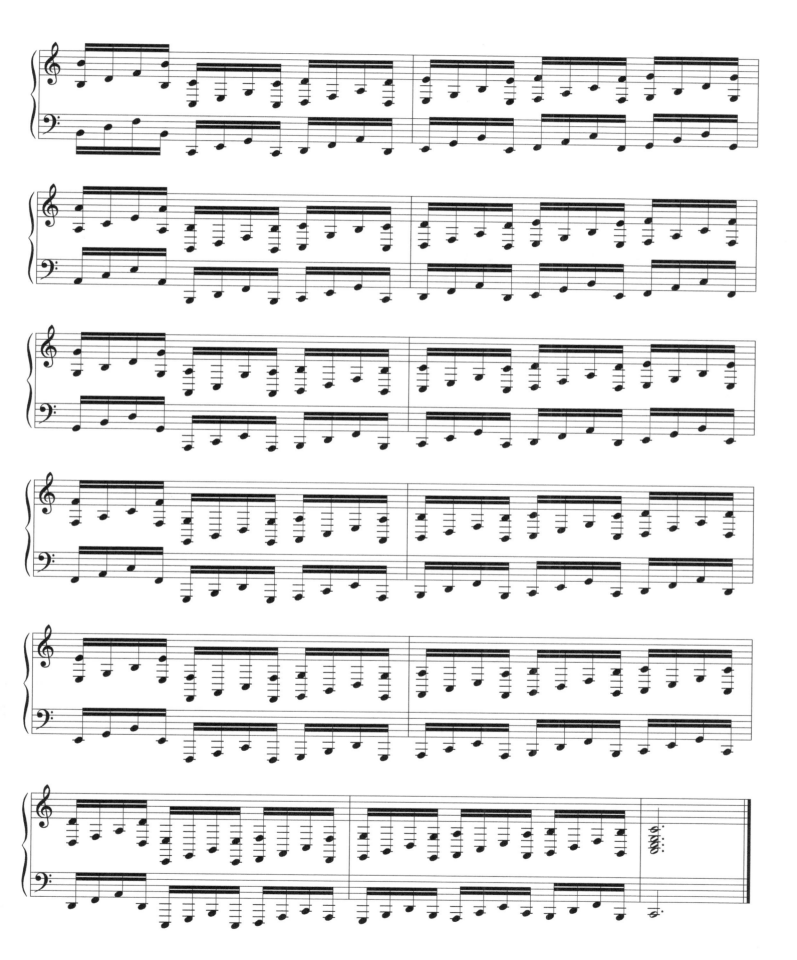

37

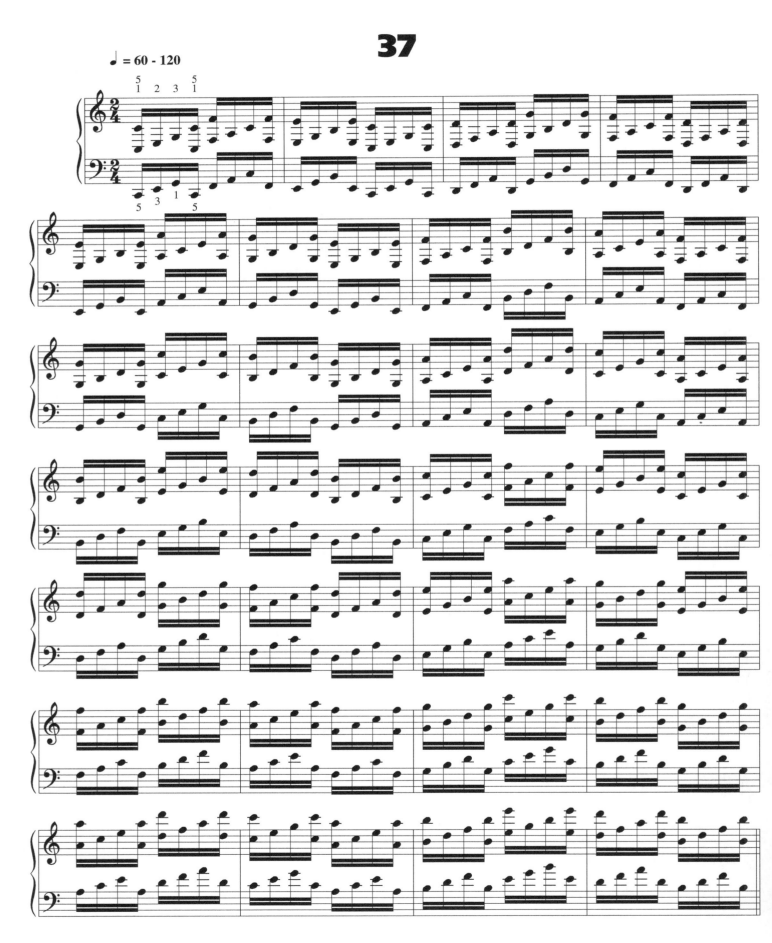

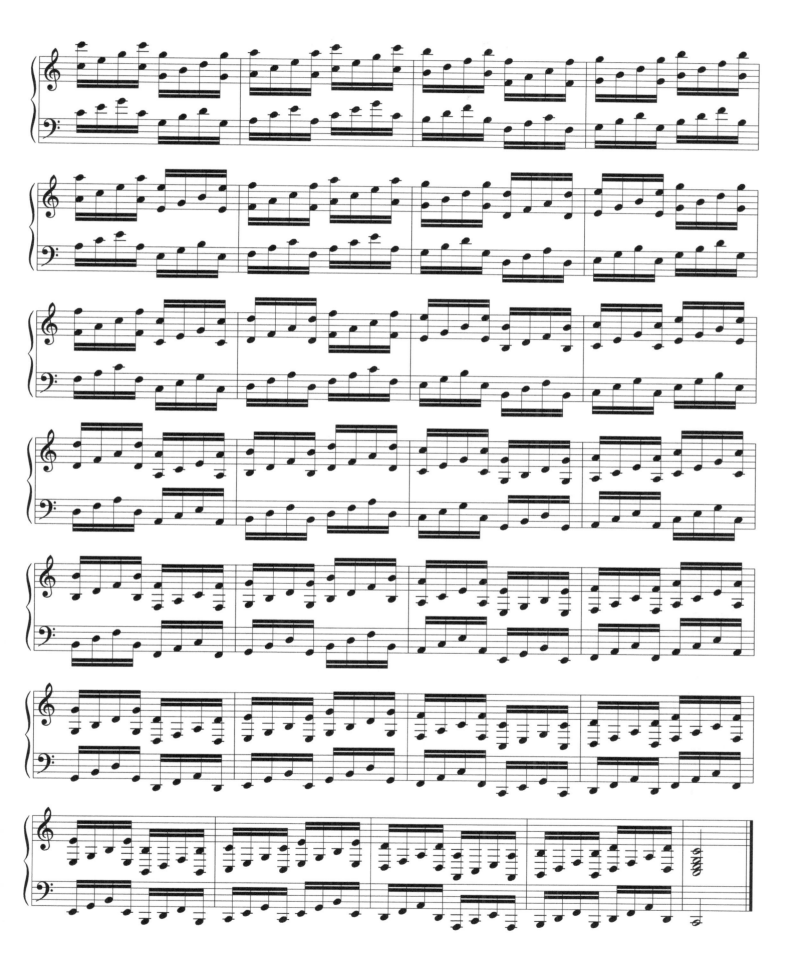

38

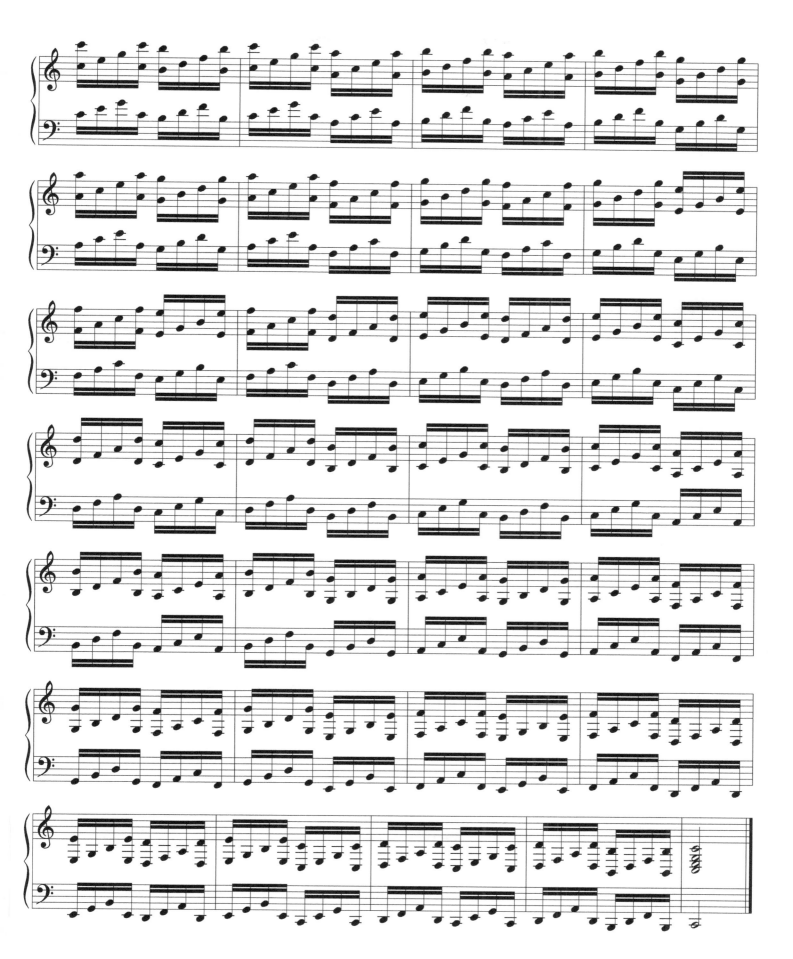

Chromatic Exercises

39

♩ = 60 - 120

40

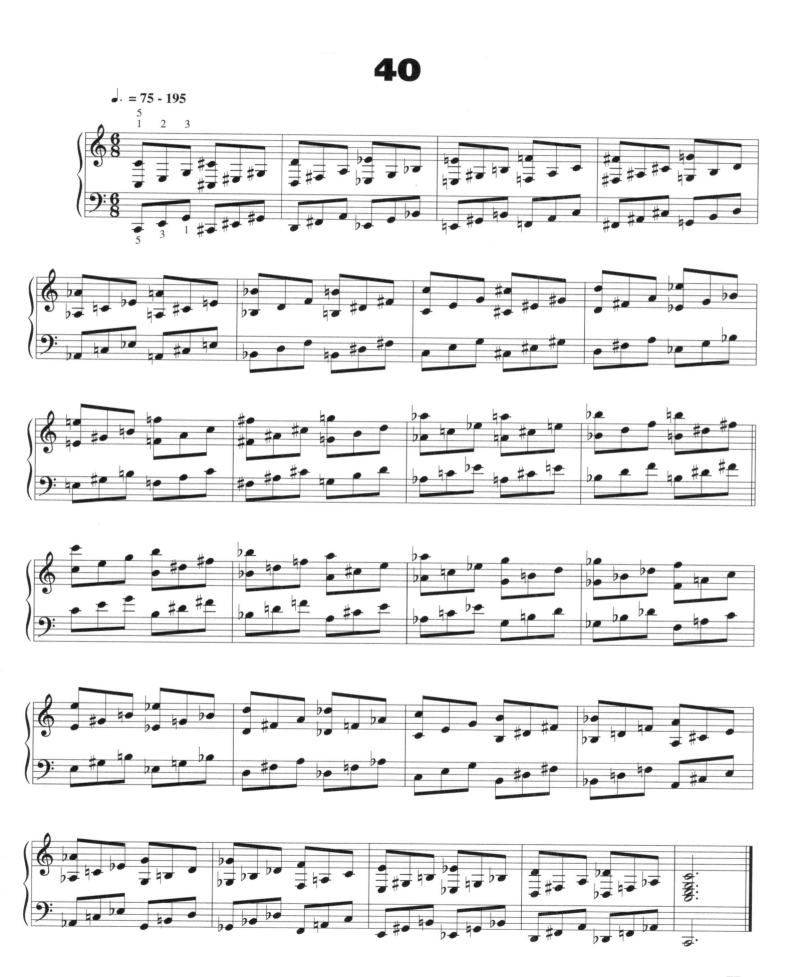

41

Syncopated Octave Montuno Exercises

42

43

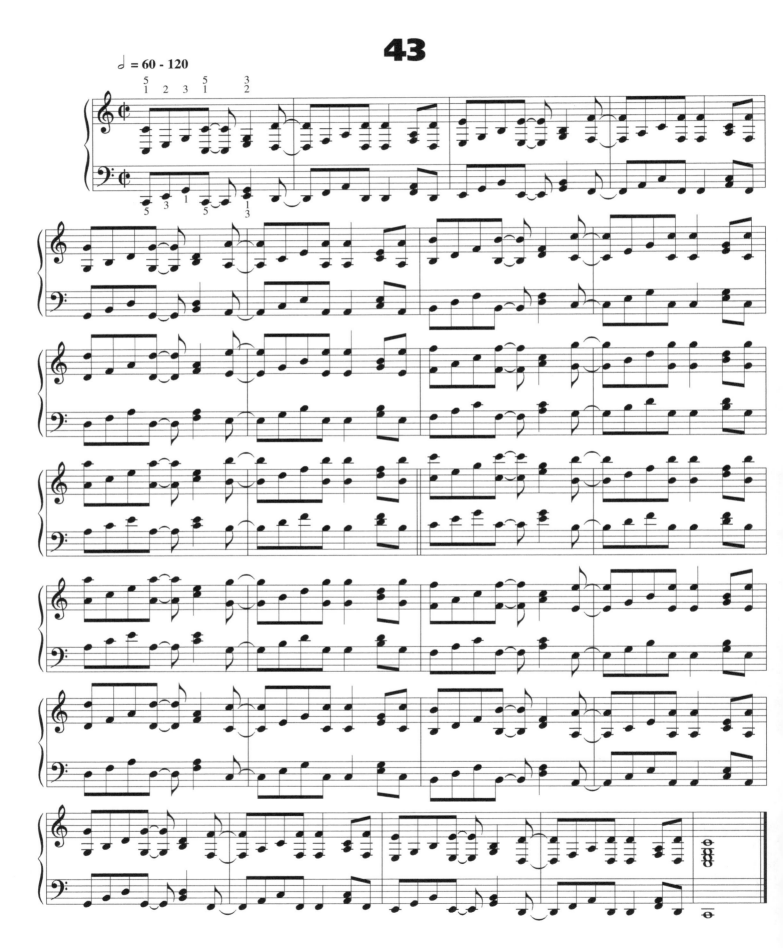

44

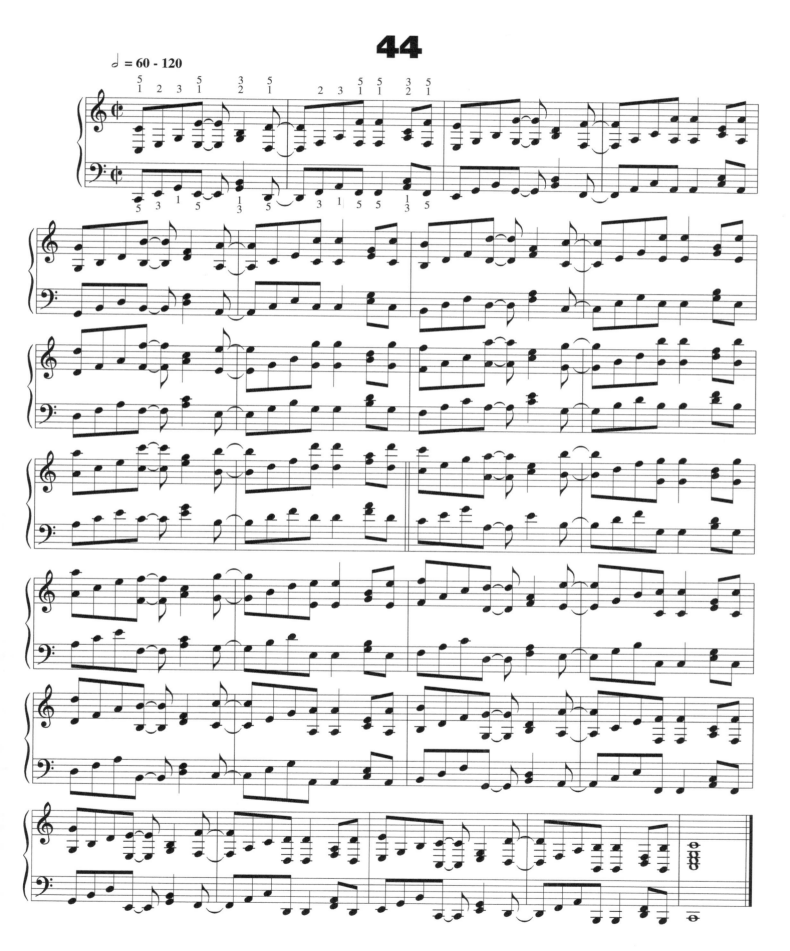

45

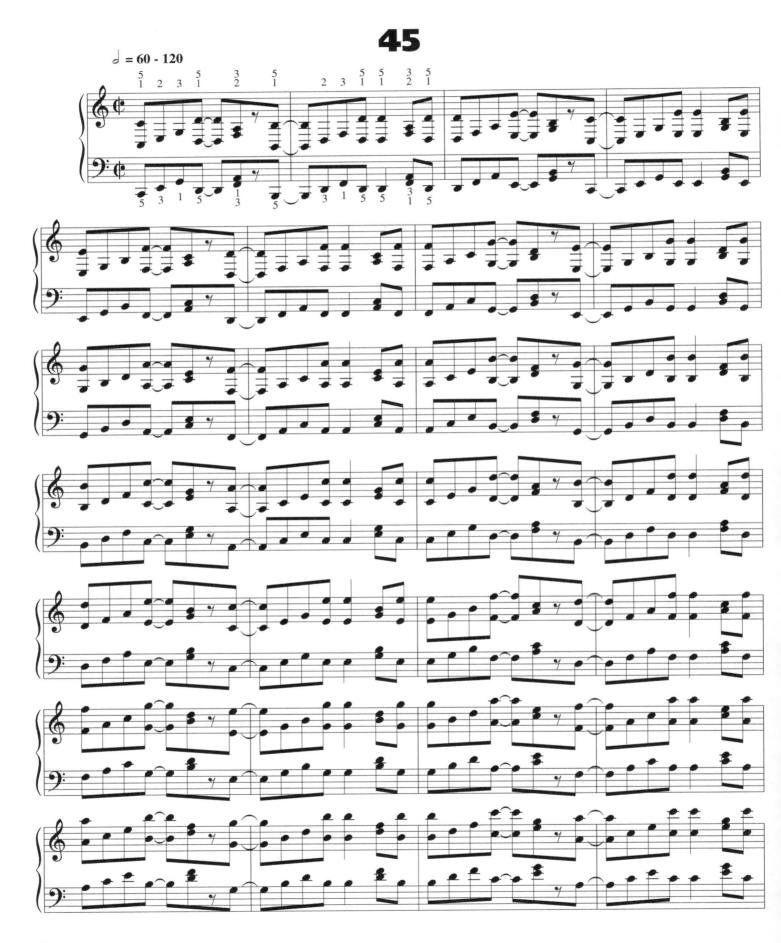

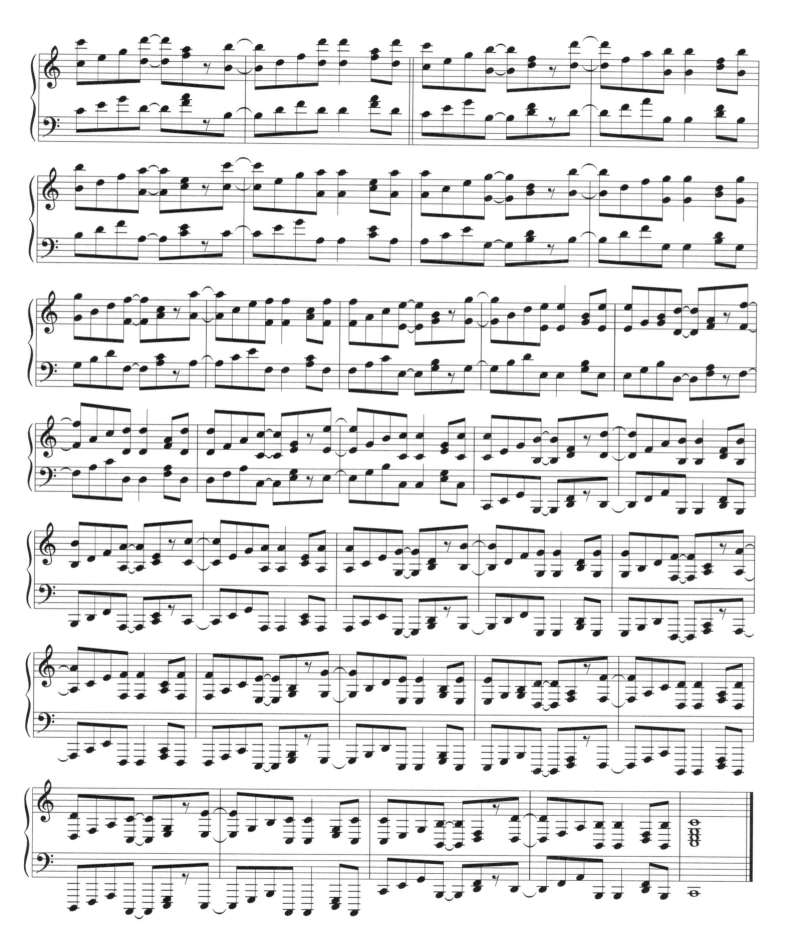

Syncopated Octave Montuno Exercise
Played Chromatically
46

Typical Latin Improvisational
Technique
47

48

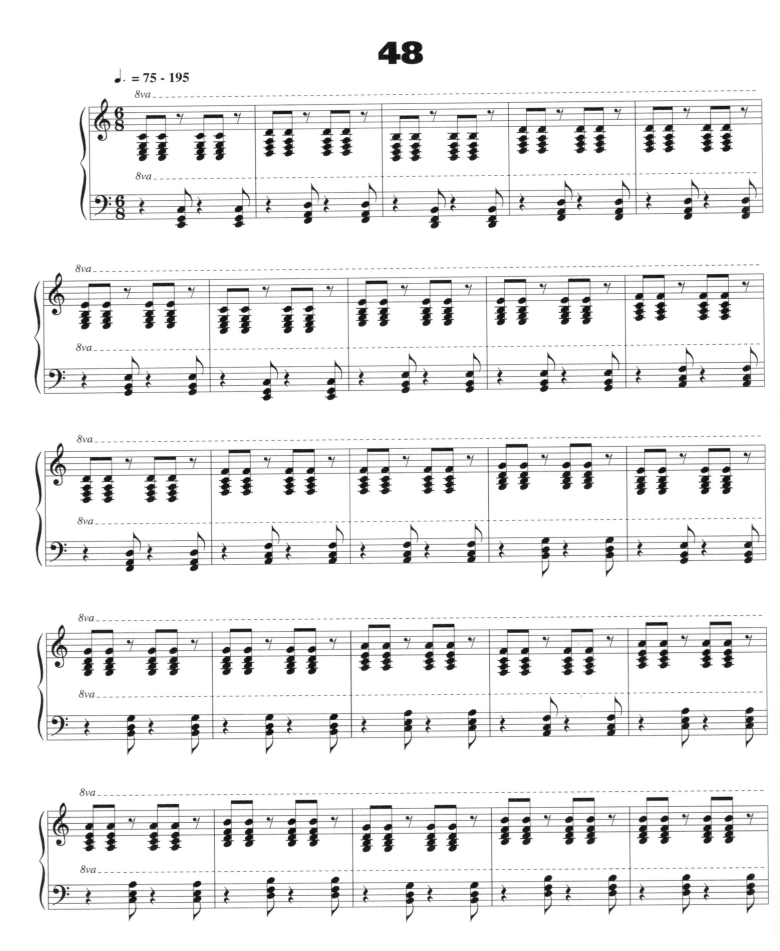

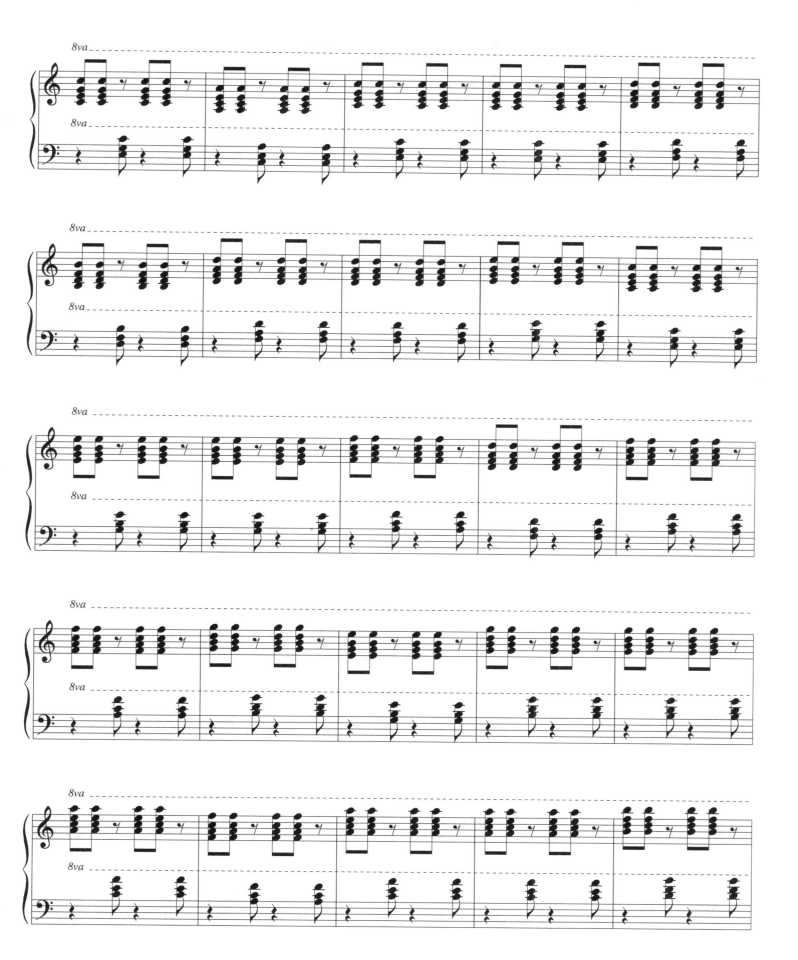

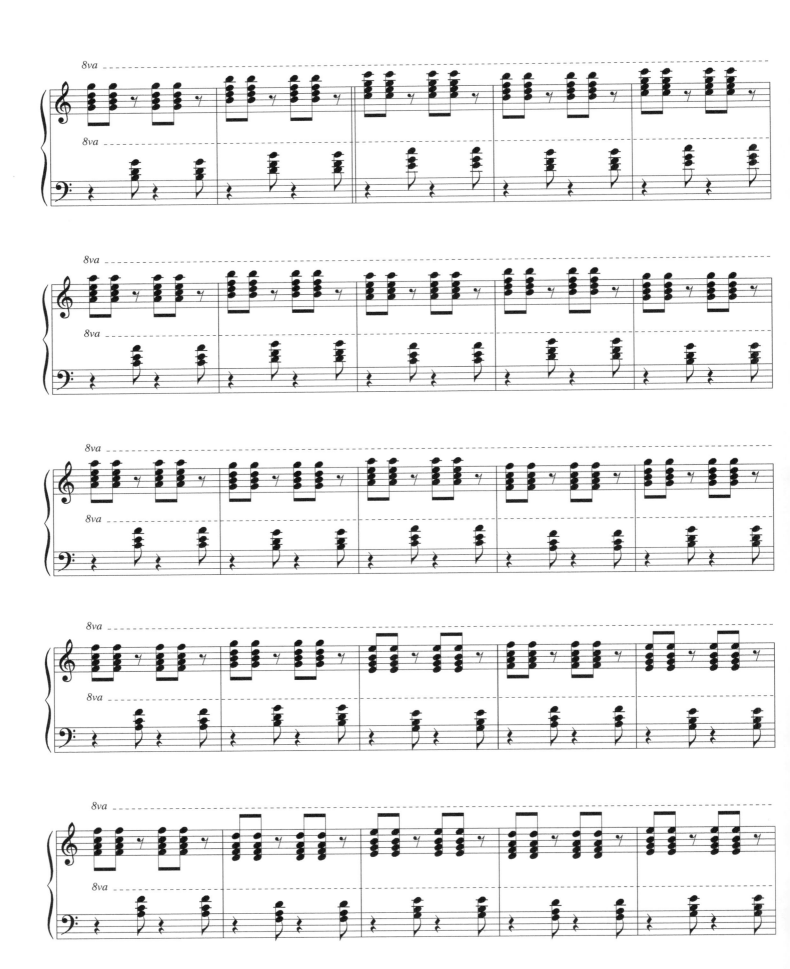

Based on a Cha-Cha Piano Rhythm

49

A Technique Common in
Cuban Piano Playing

50

Listening Guide

LATIN JAZZ

TITO PUENTE
MICHEL CAMILO
GONZALO RUBALCAVA
HILTON RUIZ
GIOVANNI HIDALGO
CARLOS "PATATO" VALDEZ
IRAKERE
PANCHO SANCHEZ
CHARLIE SEPULVEDA
ARTURO SANDUVAL
EDDIE PALMIERI
CLARE FISCHER
DANILO PEREZ

SALSA

CELIA CRUZ
OSCAR DELEON
RUBEN BLADES
MARK ANTHONY
LA INDIA

Musicians Institute Press is the official series of instructional publications from Southern California's renowned music school, Musicians Institute. These books, book/cd packages, and videos have been created by MI instructors who are among the world's best and most experienced professional musicians.

KEYBOARD

00695708	Blues Hanon by Peter Deneff	$16.95
00695556	Dictionary of Keyboard Grooves by Gail Johnson – Book/CD	$16.95
00695336	Funk Keyboards – The Complete Method by Gail Johnson – Book/CD	$15.95
00695936	Hip-Hop Keyboard by Henry Soleh Brewer – Book/CD	$17.95
00695791	Jazz Chord Hanon by Peter Deneff	$16.99
00695554	Jazz Hanon by Peter Deneff	$16.99
00695773	Jazz Piano by Christian Klikovits – Book/CD	$17.95
00695365	Keyboard Technique by Steve Weingart	$12.95
00695209	Keyboard Voicings by Kevin King	$12.95
00695205	Music Reading for Keyboard by Larry Steelman	$14.99
00695509	Pop Rock Keyboards by Henry Sol-Eh Brewer & David Garfield – Book/CD	$19.95
00695327	R&B Soul Keyboards by Henry Brewer – Book/CD	$16.95
00695784	Rock Hanon by Peter Deneff	$16.99
00695226	Salsa Hanon by Peter Deneff	$16.99
00695939	Samba Hanon by Peter Deneffs	$16.99
00695882	Stride Hanon by Peter Deneff	$16.99

VOICE

00695883	Advanced Vocal Technique by Dena Murray and Tita Hutchison – Book/CD	$19.95
00695262	Harmony Vocals by Mike Campbell & Tracee Lewis – Book/CD	$19.99
00695626	The Musician's Guide to Recording Vocals by Dallan Beck – Book/CD	$15.99
00695629	Rock Vocals by Coreen Sheehan – Book/CD	$17.99
00695195	Sightsinging by Mike Campbell	$19.99
00695427	Vocal Technique by Dena Murray – Book/2-CDS	$24.99

GUITAR

00695636	Advanced Guitar Soloing by Daniel Gilbert & Beth Marlis – Book/CD	$19.99
00695298	Advanced Scale Concepts and Licks for Guitar by Jean Marc Belkadi – Book/CD	$16.95
00695180	Basic Blues Guitar by Steve Trovato – Book/CD	$15.99
00695680	Blues/Rock Soloing for Guitar by Robert Calva – Book/CD	$19.99
00695131	Blues Rhythm Guitar by Keith Wyatt – Book/CD	$19.95
00696002	Modern Techniques for the Electric Guitarist by Dean Brown – DVD	$29.95
00695664	Chord Progressions for Guitar by Tom Kolb – Book/CD	$17.99
00695855	Chord Tone Soloing by Barrett Tagliarino – Book/CD	$24.99
00695646	Chord-Melody Guitar by Bruce Buckingham – Book/CD	$17.99
00695171	Classical & Fingerstyle Guitar Techniques by David Oakes – Book/CD	$17.99
00695806	Classical Themes for Electric Guitar by Jean Marc Belkadi – Book/CD	$15.99
00695320	Contemporary Acoustic Guitar by Eric Paschal & Steve Trovato – Book/CD	$16.95
00695172	Creative Chord Shapes by Jamie Findlay – Book/CD	$10.99
00695227	The Diminished Scale for Guitar by Jean Marc Belkadi – Book/CD	$10.99
00695181	Essential Rhythm Guitar by Steve Trovato – Book/CD	$15.99
00695873	Ethnic Rhythms for Electric Guitar by Jean Marc Belkadi – Book/CD	$17.99
00695860	Exotic Scales & Licks for Electric Guitar by Jean Marc Belkadi – Book/CD	$16.95
00695419	Funk Guitar by Ross Bolton – Book/CD	$15.99
00695134	Guitar Basics by Bruce Buckingham – Book/CD	$17.95
00695712	Guitar Fretboard Workbook by Barrett Tagliarino	$17.99
00695321	Guitar Hanon by Peter Deneff	$9.95
00695482	The Guitar Lick•tionary by Dave Hill – Book/CD	$19.99
00695190	Guitar Soloing by Daniel Gilbert and Beth Marlis – Book/CD	$22.99
00695907	Guitar Soloing featuring Daniel Gilbert and Beth Marlis – DVD	$19.95
00695169	Harmonics by Jamie Findlay – Book/CD	$13.99
00695406	Introduction to Jazz Guitar Soloing by Joe Elliott – Book/CD	$19.95
00695291	Jazz Guitar Chord System by Scott Henderson	$10.95
00695128	Jazz Guitar Improvisation featuring Sid Jacobs – Book/CD	$18.99
00695908	Jazz Guitar Improvisation featuring Sid Jacobs – DVD	$19.95
00695639	Jazz Guitar Improvisation featuring Sid Jacobs – VHS	$19.95
00695361	Jazz-Rock Triad Improvising for Guitar by Jean Marc Belkadi – Book/CD	$15.99
00695379	Latin Guitar by Bruce Buckingham – Book/CD	$17.99
00695143	A Modern Approach to Jazz, Rock & Fusion Guitar by Jean Marc Belkadi – Book/CD	$15.99
00695711	Modern Jazz Concepts for Guitar by Sid Jacobs – Book/CD	$16.95
00695682	Modern Rock Rhythm Guitar by Danny Gill – Book/CD	$16.95
00695555	Modes for Guitar by Tom Kolb – Book/CD	$18.99
00695192	Music Reading for Guitar by David Oakes	$19.99
00695505	The Musician's Guide to Recording Acoustic Guitar by Dallan Beck – Book/CD	$13.99
00695697	Outside Guitar Licks by Jean Marc Belkadi – Book/CD	$16.99
00695962	Power Plucking by Dale Turner – Book/CD	$19.95
00695601	Practice Trax for Guitar by Danny Gill – Book/CD	$17.99
00695748	Progressive Tapping Licks by Jean Marc Belkadi – Book/CD	$15.95
00695188	Rhythm Guitar by Bruce Buckingham & Eric Paschal	$17.95
00695909	Rhythm Guitar featuring Bruce Buckingham – DVD	$19.95
00695144	Rock Lead Basics by Nick Nolan and Danny Gill – Book/CD	$18.99
00695910	Rock Lead Guitar featuring Danny Gill – Book/CD	$19.95
00695278	Rock Lead Performance by Nick Nolan and Danny Gill – Book/CD	$17.95
00695146	Rock Lead Techniques by Nick Nolan and Danny Gill – Book/CD	$16.99
00695977	Shred Guitar by Greg Harrison – Book/CD	$19.99
00695645	Slap & Pop Technique for Guitar by Jean Marc Belkadi – Book/CD	$14.99
00695913	Technique Exercises for Guitar by Jean Marc Belkadi – Book/CD	$15.99
00695340	Texas Blues Guitar by Robert Calva – Book/CD	$17.95
00695863	Ultimate Guitar Technique by Bill LaFleur – Book/CD	$19.95

BASS

00695133	Arpeggios for Bass by David Keif	$14.95
00695168	The Art of Walking Bass by Bob Magnusson – Book/CD	$19.99
00696026	Bass Blueprints by Dominik Hauser – Book/CD	$18.99
00695201	Bass Fretboard Basics by Paul Farnen	$17.99
00695207	Bass Playing Techniques by Alexis Sklarevski	$17.99
00696191	Beginning Jazz Bass by Dominick Hauser – Book/CD	$19.99
00695934	Chords for Bass by Dominik Hauser – Book/CD	$17.99
00695771	Groove Mastery by Oneida James – Book/CD	$17.95
00695265	Grooves for Electric Bass by David Keif – Book/CD	$16.99
00695543	Latin Bass by George Lopez & David Keif – Book/CD	$16.99
00695203	Music Reading for Bass by Wendi Hrehhovcsik	$10.95
00696371	Progressive Rock Bass by Christopher Maloney – Book/CD	$19.99

DRUMS

00695328	Afro-Cuban Coordination for Drumset by Maria Martinez – Book/CD	$16.99
00695623	Blues Drumming by Ed Roscetti – Book/CD	$14.95
00695284	Brazilian Coordination for Drumset by Maria Martinez – Book/CD	$15.99
00695129	Chart Reading Workbook for Drummers by Bobby Gabriele – Book/CD	$16.99
00695723	Double Bass Drumming by Jeff Bowders – Book/CD	$19.95
00695869	Double Bass Drumming by Jeff Bowders – DVD	$24.95
00695349	Drummer's Guide to Odd Meters by Ed Roscetti – Book/CD	$15.99
00695986	Essential Drumset Fills by Jeff Bowders – Book/CD	$19.99
00695679	Funk & Hip-Hop Drumming by Ed Roscetti – Book/CD	$16.99
00695287	Latin Soloing for Drumset by Phil Maturano – Book/CD	$16.99
00695876	Ray Luzier – DVD	$29.95
00695755	The Musician's Guide to Recording Drums by Dallan Beck – Book/CD	$19.95
00695838	Rock Drumming Workbook by Ed Roscetti – Book/CD	$19.95
00695127	Working the Inner Clock for Drumset by Phil Maturano – Book/CD	$17.95

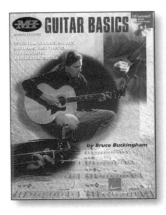 

ALL INSTRUMENTS

00695135	An Approach to Jazz Improvisation by Dave Pozzi – Book/CD	$17.95
00695136	Classic Rock Workshop Series	$19.95
00695198	Ear Training by Keith Wyatt, Carl Schroeder and Joe Elliott – Book/CD	$24.95
00695145	Encyclopedia of Reading Rhythms by Gary Hess	$19.95
00695161	Harmony and Theory by Keith Wyatt and Carl Schroeder	$19.95
00695130	Lead Sheet Bible by Robin Randall and Janice Peterson – Book/CD	$19.95

RECORDING

00695911	Home Recording Basics featuring Dallan Beck – DVD	$19.95
00695655	Home Recording Basics featuring Dallan Beck – VHS	$19.95
00695505	The Musician's Guide to Recording Acoustic Guitar by Dallan Beck – Book/CD	$13.99
00695755	The Musician's Guide to Recording Drums by Dallan Beck – Book/CD	$19.95
00695626	The Musician's Guide to Recording Vocals by Dallan Beck – Book/CD	$15.99

REFERENCE

00695322	Going Pro by Kenny Kerner – Paperback	$17.95

FOR MORE INFORMATION, SEE YOUR LOCAL MUSIC DEALER, OR WRITE TO:

HAL•LEONARD® CORPORATION

7777 W. BLUEMOUND RD. P.O. BOX 13819 MILWAUKEE, WI 53213

www.halleonard.com

Prices, contents and availability subject to change without notice.

KEYBOARD STYLE SERIES

THE COMPLETE GUIDE WITH CD!

These book/CD packs provide focused lessons that contain valuable how-to insight, essential playing tips, and beneficial information for all players. From comping to soloing, comprehensive treatment is given to each subject. The companion CD features many of the examples in the book performed either solo or with a full band.

BEBOP JAZZ PIANO
by John Valerio

This book provides detailed information for bebop and jazz keyboardists on: chords and voicings, harmony and chord progressions, scales and tonality, common melodic figures and patterns, comping, characteristic tunes, the styles of Bud Powell and Thelonious Monk, and more. Includes 5 combo performances at the end of the book.
00290535 Book/CD Pack......................................$18.95

BEGINNING ROCK KEYBOARD
by Mark Harrison

This comprehensive book/CD package will teach you the basic skills needed to play beginning rock keyboard. From comping to soloing, you'll learn the theory, the tools, and the techniques used by the pros. The accompanying CD demonstrates most of the music examples in the book.
00311922 Book/CD Pack......................................$14.99

BLUES PIANO
by Mark Harrison

With this book/CD pack, you'll learn the theory, the tools, and even the tricks that the pros use to play the blues. You also get seven complete tunes to jam with on the CD. Covers: scales and chords; left-hand patterns; walking bass; endings and turnarounds; right-hand techniques; how to solo with blues scales; crossover licks; and more.
00311007 Book/CD Pack......................................$17.95

BRAZILIAN PIANO
by Robert Willey and Alfredo Cardim

Brazilian Piano teaches elements of some of the most appealing Brazilian musical styles: choro, samba, and bossa nova. It starts with rhythmic training to develop the fundamental groove of Brazilian music. Next, examples build up a rhythmic and harmonic vocabulary that can be used when playing the original songs that follow.
00311469 Book/CD Pack......................................$19.99

CONTEMPORARY JAZZ PIANO
by Mark Harrison

From comping to soloing, you'll learn the theory, the tools, and the techniques used by the pros. The full band tracks on the CD feature the rhythm section on the left channel and the piano on the right channel, so that you can play along with the band.
00311848 Book/CD Pack......................................$17.99

COUNTRY PIANO
by Mark Harrison

Learn the theory, the tools, and the tricks used by the pros to get that authentic country sound. This book/CD pack covers: scales and chords, walkup and walkdown patterns, comping in traditional and modern country, Nashville "fretted piano" techniques and more. At the end, you'll get to jam along with seven complete tunes.
00311052 Book/CD Pack......................................$17.95

GOSPEL PIANO
by Kurt Cowling

This comprehensive book/CD pack provides you with the tools you need to play in a variety of authentic gospel styles, through a study of rhythmic devices, grooves, melodic and harmonic techniques, and formal design. The accompanying CD features over 90 tracks, including piano examples as well as the full gospel band.
00311327 Book/CD Pack......................................$17.95

INTRO TO JAZZ PIANO
by Mark Harrison

This comprehensive book/CD is the perfect *Intro to Jazz Piano*. From comping to soloing, you'll learn the theory, the tools, and the techniques used by the pros. The accompanying CD demonstrates most of the music examples in the book. The full band tracks feature the rhythm section on the left channel and the piano on the right channel, so that you can play along with the band.
00312088 Book/CD Pack......................................$14.99

JAZZ-BLUES PIANO
by Mark Harrison

This comprehensive book will teach you the basic skills needed to play jazz-blues piano. Topics covered include: scales and chords • harmony and voicings • progressions and comping • melodies and soloing • characteristic stylings.
00311243 Book/CD Pack......................................$17.95

JAZZ-ROCK KEYBOARD
by T. Lavitz

Learn what goes into mixing the power and drive of rock music with the artistic elements of jazz improvisation in this comprehensive book and CD package. This instructional tool delves into scales and modes, and how they can be used with various chord progressions to develop the best in soloing chops.
00290536 Book/CD Pack......................................$17.95

LATIN JAZZ PIANO
by John Valerio

This book is divided into three sections. The first covers Afro-Cuban (Afro-Caribbean) jazz, the second section deals with Brazilian influenced jazz – Bossa Nova and Samba, and the third contains lead sheets of the tunes and instructions for the play-along CD.
00311345 Book/CD Pack......................................$17.99

POST-BOP JAZZ PIANO
by John Valerio

This book/CD pack will teach you the basic skills needed to play post-bop jazz piano. Learn the theory, the tools, and the tricks used by the pros to play in the style of Bill Evans, Thelonious Monk, Herbie Hancock, McCoy Tyner, Chick Corea and others. Topics covered include: chord voicings, scales and tonality, modality, and more.
00311005 Book/CD Pack......................................$17.95

PROGRESSIVE ROCK KEYBOARD
by Dan Maske

From the classic sounds of the '70s to modern progressive stylings, this book/CD provides you with the theory and technique to play and compose in a multitude of prog rock styles. You'll learn how soloing techniques, form, rhythmic and metrical devices, harmony, and counterpoint all come together to make this style of rock the unique and exciting genre it is.
00311307 Book/CD Pack......................................$17.95

Prices, contents, and availability
subject to change without notice.

Visit Hal Leonard online at
www.halleonard.com

FOR MORE INFORMATION, SEE YOUR LOCAL MUSIC DEALER,
OR WRITE TO:

7777 W. BLUEMOUND RD. P.O. BOX 13819 MILWAUKEE, WI 53213

R&B KEYBOARD
by Mark Harrison

From soul to funk to disco to pop, you'll learn the theory, the tools, and the tricks used by the pros with this book/CD pack. Topics covered include: scales and chords, harmony and voicings, progressions and comping, rhythmic concepts, characteristic stylings, the development of R&B, and more! Includes seven songs.
00310881 Book/CD Pack......................................$17.95

ROCK KEYBOARD
by Scott Miller

Learn to comp or solo in any of your favorite rock styles. Listen to the CD to hear your parts fit in with the total groove of the band. Includes 99 tracks! Covers: classic rock, pop/rock, blues rock, Southern rock, hard rock, progressive rock, alternative rock and heavy metal.
00310823 Book/CD Pack......................................$17.95

ROCK 'N' ROLL PIANO
by Andy Vinter

Take your place alongside Fats Domino, Jerry Lee Lewis, Little Richard, and other legendary players of the '50s and '60s! This book/CD pack covers: left-hand patterns; basic rock 'n' roll progressions; right-hand techniques; straight eighths vs. swing eighths; glisses, crushed notes, rolls, note clusters and more. Includes six complete tunes.
00310912 Book/CD Pack......................................$17.95

SALSA PIANO
by Hector Martignon

From traditional Cuban music to the more modern Puerto Rican and New York styles, you'll learn the all-important rhythmic patterns of salsa and how to apply them to the piano. The book provides historical, geographical and cultural background info, and the 50+-track CD includes piano examples and a full salsa band percussion section.
00311049 Book/CD Pack......................................$17.95

SMOOTH JAZZ PIANO
by Mark Harrison

Learn the skills you need to play smooth jazz piano – the theory, the tools, and the tricks used by the pros. Topics covered include: scales and chords; harmony and voicings; progressions and comping; rhythmic concepts; melodies and soloing; characteristic stylings; discussions on jazz evolution.
00311095 Book/CD Pack......................................$17.95

STRIDE & SWING PIANO
by John Valerio

Learn the styles of the stride and swing piano masters, such as Scott Joplin, Jimmy Yancey, Pete Johnson, Jelly Roll Morton, James P. Johnson, Fats Waller, Teddy Wilson, and Art Tatum. This book/CD pack covers classic ragtime, early blues and boogie woogie, New Orleans jazz and more. Includes 14 songs.
00310882 Book/CD Pack......................................$17.95